BUILDING PATHWAYS TO PEACE

State–Society Relations and Security Sector Reform

Nadine Ansorg
University of Kent
Sabine Kurtenbach
German Institute for Global and Area Studies

CAMBRIDGE
UNIVERSITY PRESS

CAMBRIDGE
UNIVERSITY PRESS

Shaftesbury Road, Cambridge CB2 8EA, United Kingdom

One Liberty Plaza, 20th Floor, New York, NY 10006, USA

477 Williamstown Road, Port Melbourne, VIC 3207, Australia

314–321, 3rd Floor, Plot 3, Splendor Forum, Jasola District Centre, New Delhi – 110025, India

103 Penang Road, #05–06/07, Visioncrest Commercial, Singapore 238467

Cambridge University Press is part of Cambridge University Press & Assessment, a department of the University of Cambridge.

We share the University's mission to contribute to society through the pursuit of education, learning and research at the highest international levels of excellence.

www.cambridge.org
Information on this title: www.cambridge.org/9781009462662

DOI: 10.1017/9781009406727

First published 2023

A catalogue record for this publication is available from the British Library

ISBN 978-1-009-46266-2 Hardback
ISBN 978-1-009-40675-8 Paperback
ISSN 2515-706X (online)
ISSN 2515-7302 (print)

Additional resources for this publication at www.cambridge.org/Ansorg-Kurtenbach

Building Pathways to Peace

State–Society Relations and Security Sector Reform

Elements in International Relations

DOI: 10.1017/9781009406727
First published online: October 2023

Nadine Ansorg
University of Kent

Sabine Kurtenbach
German Institute for Global and Area Studies

Author for correspondence: Sabine Kurtenbach, sabine.kurtenbach@giga-hamburg.de

Abstract: SSR is a key element of the transitions out of war, aiming at the establishment of accountable and legitimate institutions able to prevent and sanction the use of violence. While recognizing the need to include local actors, donor policies still focus mostly on the state as a provider of security. Second generation SSR has emphasized the need to include local communities and recognize the existence of non-state actors in the provision of security and justice. However, recognition is not enough. This Element promotes a radical re-think of SSR in the context of conflict and war. Guiding question for the considerations is how can security sector reform be set up and implemented to contribute to constructive and inclusive state-society relations, and build the path to long-lasting peace? This Element argues that a focus on functional equivalents, minorities, gender, and human rights is key for the design, implementation, and success of SSR.

This Element also has a video abstract: www.cambridge.org/Ansorg

Keywords: Security sector reform, security, justice, post-war, human rights

ISBNs: 9781009462662 (HB), 9781009406758 (PB), 9781009406727 (OC)
ISSNs: 2515-706X (online), 2515-7302 (print)

Contents

1 Security Sector Reform as a Wicked Problem

Security sector reform (SSR) has become a standard component of the toolbox for interventions in conflict-affected states, and also for those states in the process of leaving behind armed conflict, violence, or authoritarian rule. While the goal of both processes may be the same – achieving a democratic and accountable security sector – and there may be significant overlap in the two processes, the contexts and underlying conditions differ in meaningful ways. Civil–military relations and democratic oversight are at the core of democratization processes (Bruneau and Matei 2008; Croissant et al. 2011; Croissant and Kuehn 2017). The context of transitions out of war or armed conflict is even more demanding, as various armed actors need to be integrated, demobilized, or dismantled and restructured (Giustozzi 2008; Sedra 2017; Berg 2020). In both contexts, SSR has often been driven and heavily funded by powerful actors from the Global North, including a variety of donors such as the World Bank, which has major implications for design, process, and implementation (OECD 2005, 2007). Afghanistan is the most recent and obvious example of how difficult this process is and how quickly it can fail. The main template has been the Western Weberian central state, although the United Nations Security Council Resolution 2151 on SSR (2014) recognizes the 'sovereign right' of the respective countries and their governments 'to determine the national approach and priorities' of this process. Security sector reform is a highly complex and often contentious process, wherein the question of who is in the driver's seat depends largely on the specific power relations within a country, the political will and the interests of its elites, as well as the economic and geostrategic interests of international organizations and bilateral donors. Security sector reform has often been criticized for being heavily driven by a Western template, but its aims address a core function of every social and political order – the provision of a minimum of security and justice to its populations. It is important to acknowledge that SSR does not necessarily reduce responsibility for security provision to the Weberian state. Security can be provided by state and non-state actors, formal and informal institutions, by using violence or by social control (Scheye and McLean 2006; Abrahamsen and Williams 2009; Meagher 2012; Albrecht and Kyed 2015; Abrahamsen 2016; Tapscott 2021). Therefore, in the present contribution, we focus on SSR in post-war and out-of-war transitions, and relations between local societies, elites, and international actors in the process.

Although there is no specific definition of SSR, its overall aim is '[to develop] an affordable, effective and efficient security apparatus' (DCAF 2006, 3) that encapsulates a functioning police force for internal security and a functioning military for external security. Broader notions of 'security governance' or 'security system' include strengthening the independence of the judiciary and the rule of law (OECD 2005; Sedra 2017; Donais and Barbak 2021). The disarmament, demobilization, and reintegration (DDR) of non-state armed groups is closely linked to SSR and is mostly a first step toward achieving it (Giustozzi 2012b; Munive and Stepputat 2015). Hence, SSR intends to be a highly transformative endeavour that aims (at least theoretically) to increase the security of the broader population and the accountability of those providing it. However, the reality often looks very different, with insecurity remaining for years, if not decades, after a war has ended, and state security forces being heavily involved in violence and crime.

Due to these difficulties, the importance of SSR for post-war countries has been widely recognized, and external donors provide substantial money, time, and expertise to support these reforms. Despite, or perhaps because of, massive funding, the problems on the ground continue to be manifold. The three most important are as follows.

(i) Despite the increasing acknowledgement of the need to develop 'local ownership' (Baker and Scheye 2007; Oosterveld and Galand 2012), it is rare for local contexts and actors to be systematically involved in post-war SSR. Security sector reform programmes continue to follow a Western state-centred blueprint whose aim is to (re-)establish a state monopoly on force – an approach that is not necessarily appropriate in the varied and disparate historical, cultural, and economic settings of the Global South (Schroeder and Chappuis 2014). Empirical evidence shows a clear gap between policy of powerful donors and practice of SSR in fragile contexts in the Global South that persists today (Albrecht and Jackson 2014; Jackson 2018; Sedra 2018).

(ii) Peacebuilding funds – specifically, funding for SSR – are overwhelmingly allotted directly to (or, at least, are mostly channelled via) the central government for the purpose of strengthening its capacities to provide security. A recent study of the United Nations University (Day et al. 2021) highlights that this may – unintentionally – support authoritarian tendencies and thus endanger peacebuilding as the governments tend to expand executive power at the expense of accountability. Despite the acknowledgement of a 'multi-layered approach to security' (Kyed and Albrecht 2015) in security questions, the focus is still very much on formal state security institutions (Abrahamsen 2016).

(iii) Security sector reform follows a temporal sequence of DDR first, reform of the armed forces and the police second, and judicial reform

> (beyond transitional justice) last, if at all. This fails to be comprehensive and often leaves the reform process incomplete and unsustainable. It becomes most obvious when donor priorities or problems on the ground shift or where reforms interact such as between the lack of judicial reform and the recycling of wartime police officers as in El Salvador (Kurtenbach 2019). Particularly in recent years, the direction of SSR has shifted towards an increased focus on stabilization and containment of threats (Clausen and Albrecht 2021). This has prioritized the management of the direct effects of war and violence and lacked the comprehensiveness needed to promote large-scale societal transformation.

Overall, SSR funded by international organizations and powerful bilateral donors tends to focus on the stabilization and protection from security threats, along with a certain sequence of reforms, without acknowledging or including underlying societal formations systematically. This often jeopardizes peacebuilding efforts and perpetuates existing power structures and inequalities that led to the outbreak of societal violence in the first place.

Approaches of a 'second-generation' SSR that have found their way into academic debates (Scheye and McLean 2006; Baker 2010; Donais 2018; Jackson 2018; Sedra 2018) include non-state security actors as part of hybrid or multi-layered security models and acknowledge the importance of civil society actors or other non-state security actors. Nevertheless, intervening powers and those funding SSR programmes continue to use the template of a Weberian state as main reference frame for security and order. Those actors beyond the state security sector are treated as mere 'add-ons' and have not been sufficiently acknowledged. Consequently, hybrid security models only extend existing models rather than fundamentally reforming them from within. This often leads to a continuation of existent challenges within SSR.

Additionally, even though the inclusion of the so-called local has led to a wider understanding of dynamics of post-war SSR and peacebuilding, it still suffers from a fundamental problem: the notion of 'the local' is an inherently Western invention that perpetuates the idea of 'the other', 'while in reality reinforcing entrenched power hierarchies and forms of exclusion' (Julian, Bliesemann de Guevara, and Redhead 2019). As Meera Sabaratnam has stressed, these ideas are deeply entrenched in Eurocentric knowledge production and continue to reproduce the stereotypes of 'us vs. them' (Sabaratnam 2013). After all, as Vivienne Jabri argued, peacebuilding – and with it SSR after war – is a project of governing populations that follows a certain norm 'constitutive of the normative ordering of the international' (Jabri 2013, 14). The aim is to make people and regions that were previously ungoverned governable

(Jabri 2013), while negating any pre-existing forms of political order. At the same time, globalization in terms of international capital, politics of structural adjustment, and direct external interventions further weakens fragile states, as they promote decentralization, privatization, and outsourcing of core state functions including violence control (Leander 2003, 2005). Thus, these policies counter or undermine the proclaimed goals of building strong and democratic states.

The recognition of local actors in reform programmes and in academic studies on the topic is often very different from their inclusion (Julian, Bliesemann de Guevara, and Redhead 2019); this recognition re-establishes patterns of Eurocentrism in knowledge and practice of SSR. If we really set out to include local actors beyond their mere recognition, we need to ensure that we start and challenge the power structures that establish the 'international–local' relationship and the categories within which the local is conceived of and constructed (Julian, Bliesemann de Guevara, and Redhead 2019, 4). Berg (2022, 195) highlighted the importance of local contexts but also observed that 'political networks and revenue constraints affect the likelihood of institutionalized security governance'. Hence, it is necessary to systematically include the power relations on the ground and their interaction with external actors in reforming the security sector.

In this Element, we tackle the challenges resulting from current policies and practices of post-war SSR in the Global South, move beyond existent models, and promote a radical re-thinking of SSR in the context of conflict and war. Rather than favouring a complete withdrawal of international actors in SSR, we argue that SSR must prioritize the security of the population (not just powerful local elites), adhering to and guaranteeing fundamental individual and collective human rights. This approach is not Eurocentric, as the international conventions on human rights were developed with the participation and sometimes even the leadership of actors from the Global South. At the same time, external actors can often serve a specific purpose as they are the ones that fund certain activities, thus supporting local actors to implement reforms, and eventually aiding the (re-)establishment of security and order in post-war countries. A guiding question for our consideration is: how can SSR be set up and implemented to contribute to constructive and inclusive state–society relations and to build the path to long-lasting peace? We analyse this question with a focus on social contracts in a society. The provision of security and the reduction or containment of direct physical violence is a key task in all societies. While the question of whether it is important to control violence is largely undisputed, the path to how this can be done, what forms of violence are considered legitimate, and who is responsible for controlling violence is highly controversial and continues to change over time. The use of violence in schools as a means to 'educate' – or, rather, control – children is a case in point. While this violence was an everyday practice across much of the world until the middle of the twentieth century, the importance of protecting children from physical harm is now increasingly acknowledged. Likewise, the control of violence exclusively by a central state and its institutions is a very specific form of the provision of security in the Global North, while in some societies functional equivalents of state institutions provide security and justice that are equally accepted by the state and society (cf. Abrahamsen 2016; Kyed and Albrecht 2015). These need to be a part of the design and implementation of SSR as much as human rights, and the inclusion of gender and ethnic minorities. Under this perspective, we focus our analysis of SSR at the interface of the relation between state and society beyond the inclusion of civil society actors and other non-state actors of security.

The following sections will provide evidence for the fruitfulness of such a state–society approach based on a multimethod research study with a statistical analysis of SSR cases worldwide, and a comparative area study (CAS) of SSR in Afghanistan and Colombia. We find that a focus on state–society relations is a fruitful and promising perspective in the analysis of SSR across a variety of social, economic, and political contexts. The translation of such an approach into policies on the ground is possible only where society has organized to advocate for, acquire, and defend their right to non-violent everyday life.

2 Security Sector Reform and State–Society Relations: A Novel Theoretical Framework

Starting from a theoretical approach to the social contract between the state and its citizens, we develop a comprehensive framework that includes several aspects of SSR (DDR, police, military, judiciary, accountability) and tackles three different aspects: (a) functional equivalents of state institutions providing security and justice, given a focus on state–society relations, such as local militias, neighbourhood groups, or traditional community authorities; (b) the importance of human rights in the provision of security and justice, as the right to physical integrity stands at the core of security; and (c) the inclusion of gender and ethnic minorities into the design and implementation of SSR. This goes beyond the current debate on a second generation of SSR as it highlights the need for an intersectional approach based on both individual and collective human rights.

In order to contribute to long-lasting peace – that is, at least a permanent reduction of violence beyond the termination of war and armed conflict – SSR not only needs to acknowledge the importance of local contexts (Schroeder, Chappuis, and Kocak 2014; Bagayoko, Hutchful, and Luckham 2016) but also requires an explicit perspective on state–society relations as a whole. In a recent study, Acemoglu and Robinson (2023) argued that state capacity is the result of power contests between elites and civil society, and that state capacity is higher in more inclusive contexts. This finding is also highly relevant for SSR. The police in particular, but also the judiciary and the military, are the most visible arms of the government (Cao and Solomon Zhao 2005). Besides the education and health sectors, which are often privatized, the most important task of a government is often considered to be the establishment of security and order in a country. However, the state security institutions are not effective in their conduct and do not provide a sufficient link to society to exercise this main task. We argue in this Element that, for security institutions to successfully exercise their duties, they need to take state–society relations into account and re-centre our thinking on people and their need for security.

Following Migdal (2001, 41–57), state–society relations can be framed as a struggle for social control between the state and a 'mélange' constituted by a variety of social formations including local power holders; political, economic, and social elites; and religious organizations. This is relevant across the globe. It is also important to note that both the state and society are highly fractionalized actors, not homogeneous ones. During wars, this fractionalization within and between state and society forms a fundamental part of a violent conflict. The focus on state–society relations is then equally important for the reconceptualization of SSR after the end of war (McCandless 2020). It moves beyond the dichotomous debates on one-size-fits-all versus localized approaches (Andersen 2011) and assesses the complex dynamics between multiple state and non-state actors of security and violence. We argue that while the normative framework of 'orthodox' SSR aims at a security sector that is 'people-centred', based on human rights and promoting democracy (Sedra 2017), realities on the ground are different. Our perspective on state–society relations does not focus on the rarely delivered normative intentions of SSR, but starts by acknowledging the often very messy realities on the ground. Thus, the concept of society is much broader than the usual claim that including civil society into SSR through capacity building enables democratic oversight and monitoring of security institutions (OECD 2007, 2005; DCAF 2019).

Putting state–society relations at the core of SSR creates a series of theoretical and policy implications. To start with, we need to reconceptualize peace and security accordingly. On this basis, we argue that a conceptual frame needs to focus more specifically on three interrelated aspects. The first is *functional equivalents* of state institutions providing security and justice, such as local militias, neighbourhood groups, or traditional community authorities that build a fundamental link between the state and citizens. The second is the *importance of human rights* in the provision of security and justice, including but also moving beyond the right to physical integrity. While the latter stands at the core of public security, the means to achieve physical integrity need to adhere to the international human rights agenda. The third aspect is the *inclusion of gender and (ethnic) minorities* into the design and implementation of SSR. Hence, SSR in post-war contexts of the Global South needs to be comprehensive, proposing that, for reform to be successful and societally accepted, the judiciary as one main pillar of accountability alongside other institutions of accountability and conflict transformation must be an integrated part, not just an afterthought. This is important in societies that do not have a functioning monopoly on violence, as the rule of law is, at least theoretically, the main link between state and society due to its everyday importance (Donais and Barbak 2021, 6).

2.1 Reconceptualizing Peace and Security

Peace is an 'elusive dependent variable' (Goertz 2020) that means many different things to many different people, which can make measurement and inclusion into analysis challenging. While the termination of war is a minimum conceptualization in research and in practice, broader notions that have shaped the international debate are related to the United Nations' Sustainable Development Goals (United Nations 2015a, 2015b, 2015c). Empirical evidence abounds that one-size-fits-all approaches to peacebuilding do not work and are actually part of the problem, as they use a minimalist concept of peace as absence of war and lack context sensitivity (Kurtenbach 2017a). For that reason, a series of new approaches to adaptive, pragmatic, illiberal, or relational peacebuilding (Piccolino 2015; Brigg 2016; de Coning 2018; Stepputat 2018; Lewis, Heathershaw, and Megoran 2018) has emerged. Others have framed peace as an everyday experience (Firchow 2018; Millar 2020; MacGinty 2021) or a multiscalar process (Millar 2021), or have analysed varieties of peace (Olivius and Åkebo 2021). At the core of all these approaches stands the acknowledgement that the interaction between actors and structures at different levels (local, sub-national, national, international) leads to very context-specific entanglements that shape the varieties of peace and the pathways towards it. At the same time, the meaning of peace is highly specific to the given cultural and historical contexts (Galtung 1981; Boulding 2000). These perceptions of peace and peacebuilding can vary in a specific context between social and political actors and may or may not be in line with approaches that external actors bring in. Thus, the challenge is to provide bridges between these meanings and the related expectations on peacebuilding. Peacebuilding also needs to integrate the different dimensions and approaches 'vertically' (McCandless, Abitbol, and Donais 2015, 3–4) by 'building effective, accountable state institutions *and* restoring social relationships, *as well as* ... linking both sets of processes'. Hence, we understand peace and peacebuilding as complex and often contentious processes (Regan 2014; Diehl 2016), whose analysis of the opportunities and the challenges must start from the relevant conflicts in a society (Kurtenbach 2020). As old conflicts persist or reproduce, new conflicts arise, which makes peacebuilding a 'perpetual' task (Paffenholz 2021).

The reconceptualization of peace has broader implications for conceptualizing security and SSR. The relationship between peace and security is historically complex and has changed in recent decades (Wæver 2003). Similar to the broader current conceptualizations of peace, security frames, at least theoretically, left behind the minimalist notion of 'national security' towards 'human or intersectional security' (Muthien 2018). This is highly relevant for SSR. If peace is not just contrary to war but to various forms of direct physical violence (Pearce 2016; Kurtenbach 2020), and the main target of security is the general population, any attempts at SSR should not only tackle war-related violence but also address multiple forms of political and societal or 'criminal' violence that fundamentally violate the social contract between the state and its people.

Controlling direct physical violence is a central task in all societies, or is at least one of the elementary core functions (Elias 1987). However, violence against some populations such as ethnic minorities, women, or children may be justified by different actors because these groups are not considered 'citizens' in their eyes and are thus deprived of the right to physical integrity and other fundamental rights (Walby 2013). The underlying mechanisms of exclusion can be observed prior to and in contexts of armed conflict and war, where these populations are framed as 'enemies' endangering the status quo of the existing order. Even if the question of how violence can be controlled may be controversial, the question of whether it is important to control violence is largely undisputed. The discussions about the legitimization of different forms of violence or their causes – for example, in the context of revolutions or insurrections – confirm this statement (Holdt 2012).

Regarding post-war contexts, research has specifically examined war recurrence (Binningsbø, Buhaug, and Dahl 2012; Call 2012; Daly 2014; Berg 2020), but is increasingly acknowledging the need to leave behind the compartmentalization of different forms of violence and pursue an integrated and comprehensive analysis (Barnes 2017; Bara, Deglow, and van Baalen 2021). There is no clear-cut boundary, either in war or in post-war contexts, between different forms of violence (Kalyvas 2006; Andreas and Greenhill 2010; Barnes 2017).

Empirical evidence shows how different forms of violence influence the overall peacebuilding process either because peacebuilding is a contentious process (Birke Daniels and Kurtenbach 2021) or via the re-traumatization of civilians and the empowerment of state and non-state armed actors (; Darby 2006; Steenkamp 2011; Kurtenbach 2013; Gartner and Kennedy 2018).

This is consequential for SSR. UN Security Council Resolution 2151 (2014) on SSR explicitly recognizes the link between SSR and armed violence reduction, as do the UN reports on sustainable peace (United Nations 2015a, 2015c). From this perspective, SSR is linked to a broader understanding of public security beyond the security of former combatants towards the general population (Call and Stanley 2001). These innovative perspectives are central to the analysis of SSR, as they highlight the political character of post-war institutional reforms.

2.2 Functional Equivalents to State Institutions

To comprehensively analyse SSR from a state–society perspective, we need to draw attention to the fact that the state is neither a homogeneous actor nor the only provider of security and justice. Particularly in areas of limited statehood, security providers are as variegated as manifestations of violence (Baker and Scheye 2007; Baker 2010; Albrecht and Kyed 2015). Critical security studies have widely acknowledged the importance of security providers beyond the state and context-specific perceptions of security (Luckham 2015, 2017; Sedra 2018; Brown 2020). Society is a social space constituted by the struggles and relationships between different social formations. Functional equivalents of state institutions are an explicit part of the landscape of a society's security and justice sector; this has either not been acknowledged or has been perceived as too challenging by international policy actors as it goes against the template of a Weberian state as the main reference frame for security and order. We define those functional equivalents as actors providing security and justice outside of the state system.

The ability of these groups to establish hierarchies, form alliances, use resources, enforce norms, and mobilize followers in a society determines power relations and their legitimacy structures (Migdal 2001, 103–10). Therefore, the state is only one of many important actors in this area, which reflects the heterogeneity and complexity of society but also influences it. This reflects realities on the ground, where, in many places, the central state is not present or even part of the contentious processes of change and transformation. This 'mélange' and the reality of 'simultaneous authority' (Albrecht and Moe 2015) in contexts often framed as hybrid or multi-layered (cf. Abrahamsen 2016) needs to be the starting point for reform including bottom-up and top-down approaches from a state–society perspective. To assess the provision of security and justice by both state and non-state institutions and actors, we ask the following question: who provides security and justice, where, for whom, and by what means? This assessment will reveal insights into the inclusive or exclusive character of SSRs and enable us to determine the conditions under which SSRs contribute to long-term peace or to fragmented and fragile peace.

The pluralization of security governance (Caparini 2006), including policing, the military, and the justice sector, has received increasing attention in the last decade and is by no means limited to the Global South or post-war contexts, but is a common feature across the globe. Empirical evidence offers an opportunity to classify these functional equivalents along (a) their relation to the state and/or civil society – that is, competition, delegation, or complementation; (b) their territorial scope (local, national, transnational); and (c) their means – that is, coercion, persuasion, or social control. None of these categories can be clearly delimited as overlaps are frequent.

There is a vivid debate about the specific characteristics of various non-state groups, the most prominent being insurgents, vigilantes, and organized crime, all of which provide security and justice governance in the territories they have major control over. What differs is their territorial scope and their relation to the state. 'Rebel governance' (Arjona, Kasfir, and Mampilly 2015) mostly competes with the state, either to substitute it or to acquire or maintain control over a specific territory. Examples are so-called liberated zones where insurgents hold power for at least some period of time, such as during the Salvadorean civil war in Chalatenango, or the Taliban in the mountains of Afghanistan (Moodie 2010; Terpstra 2020). Vigilante groups develop in the context of insecurity playing a complementary role to the state (Tapscott 2021). The Peruvian Rondas Campesinas (Schubiger 2021) is an example. Similar to vigilante groups, organized crime groups are not restricted to the context of armed conflict and provide what has been coined as 'criminal' governance (Lessing 2021). Their relationship to the state and society varies between competition, cooperation, and even capture, depending on the specific power relations between these non-state actors at the local level and involvement of the state in these activities. The level of violence involved in their activities varies according to state response and the cohesiveness of the state security apparatus (Duran-Martinez 2015). Regarding non-armed equivalents to state institutions, traditional or religious authorities are most prominent, fulfilling important services not only in dispute resolution or conflict mediation (Hohe 2003) but also in violence prevention based on social control, persuasion, or informal rules. Traditional authorities in Northern Uganda are one of many examples.

Different in some ways – because they are not embedded into society like the previously mentioned groups – are private security companies (PSCs) and external actors. The state, international actors, and influential multinational corporations with an interest in security delegate certain functions to PSCs, either inside a country (to protect economic enterprises, for example) (Argueta 2012) or internationally (such as mercenary firms fighting on behalf of a third party during war (Wagner Group in Syria) or working in military reform in the context of SSR (McFate 2016). The PSCs then complement the state in the realm of security, which often results in a militarization of societal aspects (de Groot and Regilme 2022).

Last but not least, external actors may step in either for a specific time period as, for instance, interim or transitional governments (as was the case in Kosovo (Holohan 2016) or Timor-Leste (Croissant 2006), for example) or with a longer time horizon providing security guarantees, such as the United Kingdom in Sierra Leone (Albrecht and Jackson 2014). In these cases, a foreign state or a multilateral organization (NATO, UN, ECOWAS) or its delegates replace the post-war state in some of its core functions. Regarding gross violations of human rights, the International Criminal Court fulfils a complementary function for the signatories and steps in where these states are either not able or not willing to prosecute perpetrators. However, its presence might endanger the end of war (Prorok 2017). A similar complementary function can be observed for regional human rights courts, often accessed by victims and their organizations if national judicial systems are not responsive (Huneeus 2013). Here, compliance and implementation is difficult, as these institutions mostly do not have the power to enforce their verdicts or recommendations (except for the ICC, despite its own limited power).

The brief overview above provides evidence for the pluralization of security and justice governance by local, national, and international actors (Table 1). Their repertoires to enforce rules, achieve their goals, fulfil their mandate, or pursue their interests vary. While many of these equivalents are armed, others rely on traditional legitimacy, social control, or persuasion.

2.3 Human Rights

In post-war contexts and in relation to the examination of functional security equivalents mentioned earlier, we need to give specific importance to human rights in the provision of security. First of all, gross human rights violations, such as violations of physical integrity but also restrictions on political, civil, and collective human rights, accompany war and armed conflict and limit opportunities for societal participation and advocacy. Even where the collective

Table 1 Overview on functional equivalents in the provision of security and justice

Functions	Internal actors beyond the state	Examples	External actors	Examples
Policing	Non-state armed groups (rebels and criminals)	FARC-EP in Colombia, Warlords	UN police missions or transitional authorities	Timor-Leste, Cambodia, Kosovo
	Local vigilante groups or community policing	Guardias indígenas (Colombia), Rondas Campesinas (Peru)	International PSCs	Control Risks, Blackwater
Military	Paramilitary groups	United Self-Defence Forces of Colombia (AUC Colombia)	UN peace operations	MONUSCO (DRC)
			Bilateral or multilateral missions	AMISOM (Somalia)
	Death squads	El Salvador	International mercenary groups	Wagner Group
Justice	Traditional and religious authorities	Uganda	ICC	Former Yugoslavia
	Customary courts	Guatemala	Regional human rights courts	Inter-American Court of Human Rights

violence of a war comes to an end, the right to physical integrity is not secured or protected for all parts of society (Reardon and Snauwaert 2014). Functional equivalents to the state in the provision of security can be exclusionary and even fatal for opponents – as evidenced by al-Shabaab in Somalia or the criminal gangs in El Salvador. Thus, we argue that only those alternative security actors that adhere to the universal idea and the minimum standards of human rights can create constructive state–society relations and contribute to long-lasting peace beyond the termination of war and armed conflict.

Even though there has, rightly, been considerable criticism of ‘liberal’ peace and an international debate on the universality of human rights, a comprehensive conception of peace still requires normative reference points. Human rights – both individual and equal economic, social, and cultural – are important reference points for any analysis of a volatile environment: they are considered universal, covering the rights of *all* people in a society; and they have also been signed and ratified by the overwhelming majority of governments (Sen 2001). The fact that their implementation is only partial, and that the implementation contests existing power relations is a key challenge for peacebuilding, as is the Western bias in favour of individual human rights. The possible objection that a human rights framework again follows Western blueprints can be rebutted by arguing that the formulation of universal human rights was by no means a Western project, but that actors of the Global South had a significant influence and share in it. For example, Sikkink (2014) has shown that Latin American countries were some of the main protagonists in the development of the idea of universal human rights. At the same time, there is a tendency to reduce human rights to those at the individual level (e.g., civil and political rights) and to ignore economic, social, and cultural rights of groups. External actors need a dual approach. Firstly, their policies and actions need to strictly adhere to fundamental human rights standards in order to prevent double standards or hypocrisy. This is difficult because the adherence to human rights cannot be restricted to SSR but will necessarily include other policy fields, such as economic relations and development cooperation. Secondly, cooperation with actors that do not respect fundamental human rights should be reduced to a minimum and creative ways to promote human rights should be found, such as through close cooperation, empowerment, and protection of marginalized groups and victims of human rights violations. This is not viable short-term but needs a longer commitment, as the experiences in Colombia show (Bouvier 2009). However, where there are no actors with even a minimum commitment to human rights, international actors should stay away or reduce cooperation to strictly humanitarian issues.

In post-war societies, the main focus of human rights considerations has been dealing with the past and coping with war atrocities. There has been broad but inconclusive debate on the interaction between war termination, peacebuilding, and transitional justice with the specific aim of tackling human rights violations. While some have argued that amnesties and other forms of impunity measures for perpetrators and conflict parties are a necessary evil to end war, others have argued that amnesties harm the transitions out of war (Freeman 2009; Dancy 2018; Dancy and Wiebelhaus-Brahm 2018; Daniels 2020). Following the example of countries in transition from authoritarian to democratic governments (such as Argentina in 1983/4), national or international truth commissions have been established to document war crimes and identify responsibilities. However, explicit policies of reconciliation or recompensating victims are less common, and the prosecution of perpetrators has been carried out in only few cases. A similar debate is emerging on the relation between human rights and peacebuilding agendas, particularly the question of whether human rights need to be established as a universal norm in post-war societies above any other practical considerations of post-war peacebuilding. While positive feed-back can be identified theoretically, the relation between human rights and peacebuilding is complicated and often contradictory, as the debate on peace versus justice shows (Parlevliet 2017; Prorok 2017). The concept of human rights can have various meanings, one of which refers to 'a *vision of good governance* (highlighting process matters such as participation, accountability and transparency)' (Parlevliet 2017, 341). This is highly relevant for SSR because it addresses the central means of security and justice provisions by various actors.

The reality of human rights in many post-war countries is dire. Even if we take a minimalist conception of peace as the absence of war and focus only on political and civil rights, it is not only the authoritarian or very violent post-war societies but also the 'successful' post-war societies of the early 1990s that show huge deficits in the area of human rights. In our sample of forty-two 10-year post-war episodes, only ten countries are rated 'free' (regarding political rights for at least 1 year). Only three of the ten countries are also rated free regarding civil liberties (Croatia, Israel, and United Kingdom; Serbia was rated free in civil liberties but not in political rights). Under the assumption that human rights are mechanisms of participation and accountability and thus key for governance, it becomes evident that they are also key for SSR. The inclusion of the whole set of human rights is also necessary from a peacebuilding perspective for the non-violent transformation of structural drivers of violence. Nevertheless, we need to consider that their implementation is often highly contentious and treated as an afterthought. In this context, state and non-state actors in the security sector are key to enabling or undermining non-violent conflict transformation. At the same time, a human rights framework for SSR is systematically related to strengthening both the rule of law and an independent judiciary, emphasizing the need for an integrated approach to SSR.

The evidence points to difficulties when dealing with human rights in the process of SSR. The establishment of and adherence to human rights frameworks is often only an afterthought in post-war countries, and at times not attended to at all. However, we argue that the focus on the wider society, and the inclusion and protection of all societal groups in the process of SSR, is pivotal on the pathway to peace.

2.4 Including Gender and Minorities

From a state–society perspective, with a special emphasis on human rights, the inclusion of gender and ethnic minorities into the design and implementation of SSR is key for long-lasting peace. Generally, the security sector is dominated by men and patriarchist power structures (Sjoberg 2014). Although the number of women in the judiciary and other institutions of the security sector is increasing, they are still a minority in top-ranking security sector positions such as the high courts, even in OECD countries (European Commission for the Efficiency of Justice (CEPEJ) 2018, 114). Representation and inclusion of women and minorities is important in two respects. First, the presence of these groups in parliament or other decision-making institutions matters for the codification of their rights in the legal frame. Second, representation in security sector institutions is important for the implementation of the respective laws and policies, as well as for changes in behaviour. This is even more the case in post-war societies in which ideas of toxic masculinity abet both the recruitment of combatants and overall violence against large parts of society. To counter these toxic conditions in the security sector, both international and local actors see the inclusion of aspects of gender into reform programmes as increasingly important (True and Parisi 2013; Ansorg and Haastrup 2018). Strategies including hiring women into domains typically dominated by men to strengthen the role of women and femininity while promoting women's contributions as distinct, accounting for the complexity of gender relations (cf. True and Parisi 2013). Given the path dependency of security institutions in post-war societies, gender mainstreaming is hardly ever carried out radically in that it completely overturns existing patriarchal structures. Instead, change often happens in small, nonlinear steps. This became evident during police reform efforts in Afghanistan, where the more active participation of women in the security sector was prioritized at the outset of the international mission. The gender mainstreaming in the Ukraine during the 2010s, on the contrary, was largely driven by feminist actors from within Ukrainian society. With the appointment of Ekaterine Zguladze as first deputy minister of internal affairs of Ukraine, gender practices and norms within the Ukrainian police force fundamentally changed (Ansorg and Haastrup 2018, 1135).

Particularly in deeply divided societies with complex or overlapping ethnic cleavages, SSR often aims to mirror the given society in order to integrate all ethnic or societal groups into the security forces, often under the auspices of an international peacekeeping force. In Bosnia, the UN administration introduced ethnic quotas to ensure representation of all three minority ethnic groups in the security forces (Collantes-Celador 2006, 60 f.). However, this has occasionally led to antagonism or discrimination against new colleagues, and some posts remained unfilled as no officer from the targeted ethnic group could be found for a particular region.

Equal ethnic representation can make a fundamental difference to the perception of safety in post-war countries. In Kosovo, for example, the inclusion of ethnic minorities in the police, judiciary, and so-called municipal community safety councils increased the perception of safety among respondents in the surveyed municipalities (Gray and Strasheim 2016). However, the data show that it is not only about hiring ethnic minorities. Factors such as education, training, language, prejudice, and cost can be potential challenges to the inclusion of ethnic minority groups in the security sector. Representation of ethnic minorities, or even of former combatants who are seen as adversaries of the government, is of great importance in a post-war country. At the same time, this is one of the most contentious issues, as it often means inviting antagonism into the centre of the security services, and must therefore be accompanied by careful training and educational measures.

2.5 Security Sector Reform at the Interface between State and Society

Based on the considerations about the importance of state–society relations for SSR outlined above, the analysis of SSR processes in its four elements needs a broader focus.

Regarding the DDR of former combatants, a state–society perspective must include the whole range of non-state armed actors in the analysis as well as in the related policies and reintegration. This includes a holistic analysis of the relation between armed actors and society, as well as of the relations in and with the communities that reintegrate former combatants. Recent empirical evidence shows three major deficits. First, DDR initiatives rarely include non-state armed actors beyond those that signed a peace agreement (guerrilla groups, insurgents). Demands for the inclusion of other armed actors, such as non-state militias, form part of the second-generation SSR focus on hybrid security. Recent empirical evidence shows the conditions under which militias (pro- as well as anti-government) or local self-defence groups play a major role in post-war (in)security (Munive and Stepputat 2015; Carey and González 2020; Bolte, Joo, and Mukherjee 2021). Second, from a social cohesion and integration perspective, most DDR programmes focus on individual fighters and their demilitarization and demobilization, disregarding important social bonds and relations at the group level. Governments and donors fear the persistence of wartime bonds and their potential role for remobilization (de Vries and Wiegink 2011). Lastly, reintegration needs to focus on broader livelihoods and social integration beyond cash transfers or training (Subedi 2014; Kaplan and Nussio 2018). Hence, from a state–society relations perspective, (re-)integration must focus more broadly on community building. The most important questions are: How can former combatants overcome their stigmatization or marginalization? How can programmes of economic and social (re-)integration avoid generating benefits for taking up arms? How can 'violence specialists' survive without the use of arms? And how can wartime bonds be transformed into constructive processes of building social cohesion?

A state–society approach to the reform of the *armed forces and the police* must complement the traditional emphasis on mandate, oversight, and efficiency with an analysis of the mobilization and social recruitment strategies. Functional equivalents to the state provision of security and justice need to be included in a comprehensive reform process. The representation and inclusion of women as well as ethnic minorities and other marginalized groups is an important issue (Valasek 2008; Ansorg and Gordon 2019; Gordon, McHugh, and Townsley 2021). Key elements regarding the everyday functioning of the armed forces and the police for their relations with the society and the generation of trust and legitimacy are accountability and respect for human rights. This is a main deficit of police forces across the world, as the global Black Lives Matter movement has shown. Empirical evidence shows that even police reforms from scratch – that is, the abolition of existing police forces and the establishment of completely new institutions in their place – are highly dependent on the societal context (Neild 2001). Trust in the force is a long-term endeavour and can be built only in conjunction with a holistic approach to governance and accountability to increase the legitimacy of the armed forces (Goldsmith 2005; Cruz 2015). With a focus on state–society relations, the police forces are the most visible arm of the state at different levels and must therefore address the broader panorama of public security with a special emphasis on violence prevention, protection, and conflict transformation instead of repression. State institutions also need to clarify their relation to non-state equivalents, as these can either be complementary or contest state authority and thereby produce new conflicts.

Judicial reforms in most post-war societies are reduced to the important topic of coping with past war atrocities. This may have a retributive or restorative function for delegitimizing the use of violence (Kim and Sikkink 2010) and prevent the recurrence of collective violence. Nevertheless, broader policies to promote human rights, accountability, and the rule of law are necessary as they serve as a central frame for state–society relations (Donais and Barbak 2021) and are vital for other post-war reforms. Without an effective judiciary and the political will to bring perpetrators of violence amongst the different armed forces to court, impunity will prevail and undermine other reforms. El Salvador is a paradigmatic case that shows how a lack of judicial reforms jeopardizes societal peace and, as we can currently observe, also democracy (Kurtenbach 2019). At the same time, mechanisms of vertical or horizontal accountability might vary and include both formal and informal institutions, the latter mostly at the community level.

In sum, we argue that in order for SSR to establish peace in post-war societies, we need to apply a holistic, intersectional approach that does not exclusively focus on conflict parties and combatants, but instead takes the whole of society into account and looks at the dynamics between the security sector actors, war parties, and functional equivalents of state security institutions, as well as the wider community that is affected by ongoing violence and disorder (see Figure 1).

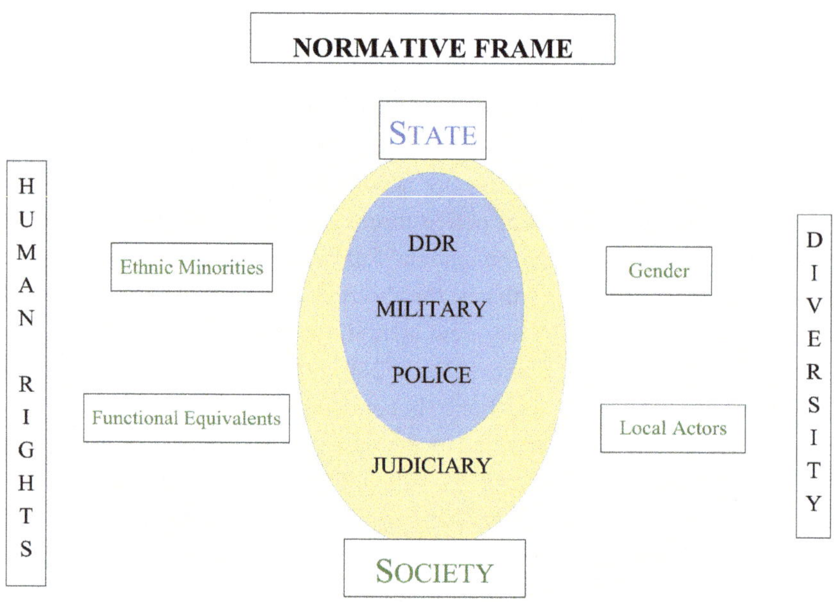

Figure 1 SSR under a state–society perspective

Source: Author's own elaboration

It is important to prioritize a human rights approach that centres on the protection of human and civil rights within the security sector. This is strongly connected to the inclusion of marginalized genders and (ethnic) minorities into the design and implementation of SSR. Finally, we also propose moving beyond a measurement of peace as the mere absence of war, incorporating other forms of violence that might have implications for security and order in a society. This is a normative approach with a long-term perspective, but as Louise Andersen (2011, 16) rightly observed, peacebuilding and institutional reforms are 'intrinsically political' and 'lasting "solutions" emerge as the unintended consequences of social processes of negotiation, contestation, and adaptation, rather than as a causal outcome of certain inputs'.

3 A Mixed-Methods Approach

To address the question of how SSR can be set up and implemented to contribute to constructive and inclusive state–society relations, and build the path to long-lasting peace, we apply a mixed-methods research design. We conducted a quantitative study on various aspects of SSR and their effect on the survival of peace using a minimalist notion as the non-recurrence of armed conflict. As this does not enable us to analyse the outlined broader notions of peace as violence reduction, we complement this with a qualitative comparison of two cases from different world regions. The use of different methods enables us to make use of the advantages, while addressing the weaknesses of each method. In particular, it enables us to include in-depth case evidence on the specific causal relations, while also generating generalizable findings on the impact of SSR on long-lasting peace. Furthermore, in the case of convergence of the results from both the qualitative and quantitative components, this could enable us to make more valid inferences.

We first examined the determinants of the security sector quantitatively. Previous research (Walter 2002; Hartzell and Hoddie 2007; Mattes and Savun 2009) has shown that peace is more likely to be established if there is commitment from the former warring parties in the form of a formal peace agreement. Therefore, we focused our analysis on the peace accords included in the Peace Accord Matrix (PAM) (Joshi, Quinn, and Regan 2015). The PAM database collates qualitative and quantitative longitudinal data on the degree to which the provisions found within thirty-four comprehensive intrastate peace agreements negotiated between 1989 and 2012 were implemented in the decade following the signing of the respective accord. The PAM defines a provision as 'a goal-oriented reform or stipulation that is costly to one or both actors, falling under relatively discrete policy domain'. There are three levels of implementation of provisions:

minimal implementation means there 'has been some effort made by the government and/or parties toward implementation but these efforts remain far short of what could be perceived as viable progress'; intermediate implementation 'refers to any amount considered viable, but short of full implementation'; and full implementation means that 'the remaining amount would not be seen as adversely affecting the viability of the process and all parties would anticipate a completed process'.

For our purposes, we use the quantitative longitudinal data specifically, and here the provision and implementation of aspects of the security sector. These are: military reform, police reform, judiciary reform, reintegration of combatants, paramilitary groups, and the presence of a UN peacekeeping force (Joshi, Quinn, and Regan 2015). These are defined and measured as follows:

- Military reform: 'The accord calls for changes in the structure, leadership, or composition of the national armed forces, changes in training procedures; civilian control over the use of the military; the integration of opposition troops into the national army.'
- Police reform: 'The accord calls for changes in the structure, leadership, or composition of the police force; changes in training procedures; civilian control over the police; the integration of opposition troops into the police.'
- Judiciary reform: 'Reforming the process of appointing or electing judges, the general criminal or civil justice system, or issues of group representation in the judiciary.'
- Reintegration: 'Programs under which ex-combatants receive job training, education, or compensation to assist them in their reintegration back into civilian life.'
- Paramilitary groups: 'Language involving the regulation and treatment of paramilitary groups including militias and mercenaries.'
- UN peacekeeping force: 'The accord calls for the deployment of a United Nations peacekeeping force to assist in stabilizing the country.'

To investigate whether SSR contributes to constructive and inclusive state–society relations and builds the path to long-lasting peace, we conducted a survival analysis with a Cox proportional hazards model.[1] The dependent variable in our analysis is the survival of peace, or the outbreak of armed conflict

[1] Survival analysis is apt for analysing smaller samples (cf. Hartzell and Hoddie 2003; Mattes and Savun 2009), which each have fewer than fifty cases in their sample. This is also because survival analysis usually has more information on a dependent variable than, for example, in logistic regression analysis with a binary outcome.

as defined by the UCDP conflict dataset (twenty-five battle-related deaths). While this might only be a rough measure of sustainable peace, as outlined above, it is a central element for an overall reduction of violence. Survival of peace is measured as the time until peace breaks down after a peace agreement and conflict recurs. Therefore, the starting time for the analysis is the day of the peace agreement. The end time is either the recurrence of conflict or – if there is no recurrence – 29 June 2022. The data of the start and end times were taken from the UCDP Peace Agreement Dataset (Högbladh 2011), the UCDP Conflict Termination Dataset (Kreutz 2010), and the Power-Sharing Event Dataset (Ottmann and Vuellers 2015). The sample is right-censored, which means we only looked at cases until 29 June 2022 and that the cases are still 'alive' (peaceful) even after the study has ended. We are aware that these quantitative data on violence are just a first indicator of sustainable peace. However, if collective violence does not end, a broader peace process including the reduction of other manifestations of violence, such as gender violence, is rather unlikely.

Our independent variables are provisions of SSR and their implementation, as outlined above. We also added several control variables to the statistical analysis. First, we followed scholarly convention to control for the level of conflict intensity (Hartzell, Hoddie, and Rothchild 2001, 205). We added the measure on the cumulative intensity of the UCDP/PRIO armed conflict database (UCDP 2013), which is a dummy variable that is '1' as soon as an armed conflict has resulted in more than 1,000 battle-related deaths over time. Second, past research found that intrastate conflict over territory results in more stable peace compared to armed conflict over government because a government may be more willing to make concessions if a fight is only over parts of a state territory, not all of it (Svensson 2009; Flores and Nooruddin 2012). To capture incompatibility, we again used data from the UCDP/PRIO armed conflict dataset (Gleditsch et al. 2002a; Themnér and Wallensteen 2012). Third, many scholars have argued that ethnic conflict is less conducive for peace than conflict over non-ethnic issues, as violence exacerbated by ethnic divisions makes peaceful coexistence and cooperation difficult (Lake and Rothchild 1996; Doyle and Sambanis 2000; Walter 2002). To capture the ethnic issue of a conflict, we use data by Walter (2004) and Kreutz (2010), who coded all cases as conflict over ethnic issues where 'combatants broke down along ethnic lines, or a faction defined itself as a separate ethnic group' (Walter 2004, 376). As this data is only available until 2006 and not all of the cases are covered by the dataset, we coded the missing cases using the same coding rules.

We also collected data on justice sector governance and reform (JSGR) across forty different post-war countries from 1990 to 2016. The JSGR dataset aims to facilitate the study of the nature and scope of post-war judicial reform and the stability of peace. In this dataset, systematic information on the following areas of the justice sector and its reform is collated: *(a) Representation* – how representative is the justice sector of the whole society? *(b) Independence* – how independent is the justice sector of political and private influence? *(c) Presence* – how accessible is the justice sector to all parts of the society? *(d) Scope* of the justice sector and its reform – does the justice sector have universal scope in the society? The JSGR explicitly focuses on aspects of governance – the conduct and management of the judiciary – including representation, independence, presence, and scope of the judiciary, and the reform efforts undertaken in these areas.

The unit of observation of the JSGR dataset is a country-year. To determine the universe of cases and our case selection, we drew on existing data collections such as the Uppsala Conflict Data Program (UCDP). We included all post-war countries in the analysis that saw a culmination of a civil conflict, which is defined as more than 1,000 battle-related deaths (BRD) in a country-year or more than twenty-five BRDs in two consecutive years (based on the UCDP dataset, cf. Gleditsch et al. 2002b; Pettersson, Högbladh, and Öberg 2019). This selection strategy resulted in a total of 40 post-war episodes, with a total of 407 country-year observations. This selection strategy enabled us to not only include cases that saw a peace agreement (as in the PAM), but also others that saw a reduction of violence by other means.

In a second step, we verified our statistical findings and explored causal mechanisms with the help of a CAS approach. The rationale of the CAS approach is to take account of the depth of local contexts and local expertise far beyond a broad overview, while using the comparative method to detect causal linkages that might travel across world regions (Köllner, Sil, and Ahram 2018). These findings can then contribute to further knowledge and insights into more general concepts and theoretical debates of certain topics, as in our case on SSR and state–society relations.

The present study was interested in evidencing similarities and differences of SSR cross-regionally, and the impact on the outcome of peace. Two cases are of particular relevance here, while others are consulted as illustrative evidence. First, we examined state–society relations in Colombia, where the violent struggle of disputes between societal groups and governments over the power and control in the country has dominated the political, economic, and social landscape for the last several decades. The Colombian war was the longest in Latin America, reflecting the major elements of war in the region; that is, a high level of social inequality, incompatibility on government, war economy structures, and an ambivalent form of formal democracy providing at least some space for civil society actors. While past reforms have been accompanied by conflict and violence, present-day Colombia serves as a case study for the interaction between a legal frame empowering civil society, on one hand, and a complex process of civil societal actors re-negotiating their place and leadership in reforms of security governance and its institutions, on the other.

Contrary to that, we also looked at the most recent example of Afghanistan, where we can see a process that was heavily driven by outside forces and was never accepted by large parts of Afghan society. While not necessarily representative of only the Middle East or South Asia, the country resembles a variety of features and problems of both regions; that is, the importance of local power holders, ethnic fragmentation, long-standing experience with external interventions. Afghanistan is the epitome of an SSR model that does not speak to historically, culturally, and economically different settings in the Global South and prioritizes government interests over local concerns. The case also evidences that a military and heavy footprint approach does not work, even in the short term, if there is no buy-in from national elites and local communities.

Both cases provide important insights into the process and conduct of SSR in post-war countries, and how it is situated within a wider societal context. In particular, we assess the involvement of both local and external actors in the reforms and determine the effect on longer-term peacebuilding. It is important to note that we not only look at the reforms per say, but analyse how they are situated within a wider context of the political regime and societal change.

Our comparison loosely applies Mill's methods of comparison (cf. George and Bennett 2005) and analyses a variety of variables that have an effect on the outcome – post-war peace. Both countries have a similar history in terms of length and intensity of violence. They both evidence high levels of subnational variation of security and justice provision by actors alongside the state and a historic lack of a state monopoly of force, as well as a profound war economy. In terms of SSR, there is a substantial difference between the two countries when it comes to engagement of wider societal actors and the holistic implementation of the reform efforts. However, we acknowledge that the two case studies are not perfectly (dis-)similar, which is why we focus on the causal process of reform situated in the societal context over a long period of time.

In the analysis, we trace the process along the four parts of SSR (DDR, police, military, and judicial reform) while emphasizing the elements highlighted in our conceptual frame: the inclusion of society, and specifically women and ethnic minorities; the importance of human rights and violence reduction; the existence and inclusion of functional equivalents into the reform process; and the role of external actors.

With the help of these cross-regional case studies, we were able to evidence how functional equivalents of state institutions need to be included in peacebuilding, particularly in areas where statehood is only limited. At the same time, we make the argument that the adherence to basic human rights is fundamentally important to avoid the creation of an authoritarian peace, or peace that is merely the absence of war, but contains other manifestations of violence.

4 Quantitative Study: Provisions and Implementation of Security Sector Reform after War

The PAM includes information on the provisions of SSR, as well as their implementation in the first 10 years after the peace agreement. In our sample, we have 323 observations as post-accord country-years. Out of these, 111 observations saw a recurrence of violence, while 212 did not see a recurrence of violence. Of the cases that saw a recurrence of violence, 34 per cent (thirty-eight observations) were scenarios in which the incompatibility concerned territory, whereas 66 per cent (seventy-three cases) concerned a fight over government. Among these cases that saw a recurrence of violence, 22 per cent (twenty-four observations) did not have an ethnic component to the conflict, whereas 78 per cent (eighty-seven observations) did. The thirty-four peace accords are regionally situated within thirty-one different countries, with the majority (fifteen, or 48 per cent) of the cases being in Africa, followed by nine (29 per cent) in Asia, four (13 per cent) in Europe, and two (6 per cent) in Latin America.

Table 2 presents summary statistics for the main variables on the implementation of SSR provisions, and the cross-tabulation with the dependent variable, recurrence of armed conflict. Military reform, police reform, and integration of combatants are the areas where we see the most implementation (also resulting from more provisions tackling these areas, not reported in this table). We see very little implementation (again resulting from few provisions) in areas such as judiciary reform, regulation of paramilitary groups, or the presence of a UN peacekeeping force.

In our survival analysis of the reform provisions, with recurrence of armed conflict as the dependent variable, we looked at different provisions on SSR and their effect on the survival of peace. We also included control variables such as ethnic conflict, previous democracy, incompatibility, and cumulative measures of conflict intensity. Out of the SSR provision variables, only provisions on the regulation of paramilitary groups have a significant and negative effect on recurrence of violence, which means that if a peace accord has provisions on the regulation of paramilitary groups, violence is less likely to recur. Out of the control variables, only incompatibility and cumulative conflict show some significance – however, this is not robust across all modules. Given that both

Table 2 Summary statistics for the implementation of security sector reform provisions

		No. Conflict recurrence, in %	Conflict recurrence, in %
Implementation military reform	0	18	15
	1	11	3
	2	21	7
	3	15	10
Implementation police reform	0	22	25
	1	5	2
	2	22	3
	3	17	4
Implementation judiciary reform	0	37	26
	1	7	3
	2	10	4
	3	12	1
Implementation reintegration	0	21	12
	1	8	6
	2	18	12
	3	19	4
Implementation regulation paramilitary groups	0	31	26
	1	2	2
	2	15	2
	3	17	5
Implementation UN peacekeeping force	0	44	23
	1	0	0
	2	2	2
	3	19	10

appear together with the variable on provisions of paramilitary groups, there seems to be some kind of interaction effect between the three variables.

Figure 2 shows the coefficient plot with provisions on paramilitary groups as well as the control variables. Provisions on paramilitary groups and previous experience with democracy are both negatively correlated with the recurrence of armed conflict, which means that a recurrence is less likely.

Next, we did a survival analysis of the implementation of reform provisions, with recurrence of armed conflict as dependent variable. In this part of the

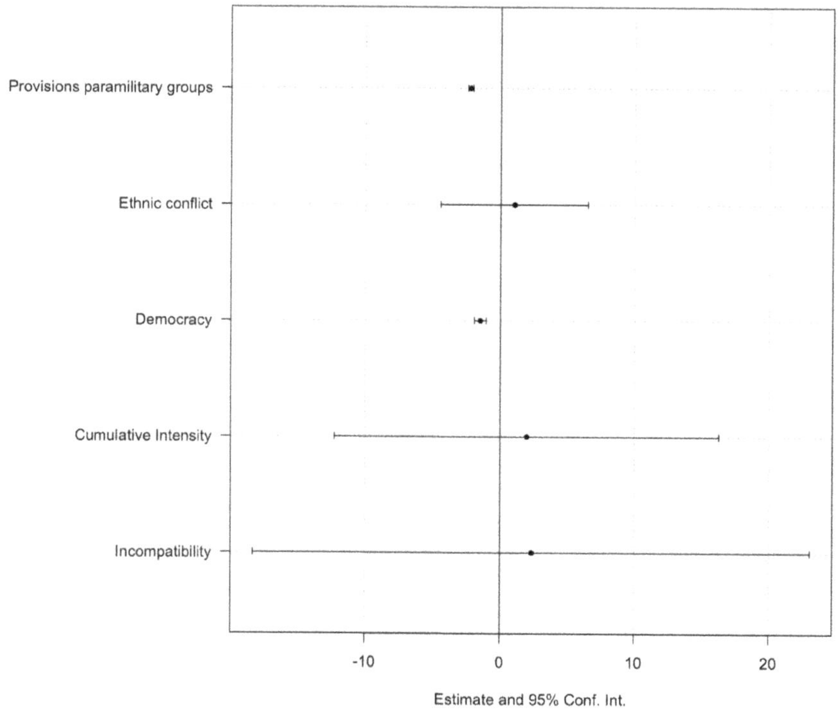

Figure 2 Coefficient plot of provisions on paramilitary groups

analysis, we analysed the implementation of SSR provisions for up to 10 years after the accord was agreed upon, and their effect on the survival of peace. Again, we included control variables such as ethnic conflict, previous democracy, incompatibility, and cumulative measures of conflict intensity.

Here it is mainly the implementation of police reform provisions, and regulations on paramilitary groups that have a significant and negative effect on the dependent variable. That means that in cases where there is an implementation of police reform provisions, a recurrence of armed conflict is less likely. Likewise, the implementation of regulations on paramilitary groups is also correlated with a smaller probability of a recurrence of violence.

Of the control variables, it is again the incompatibility variable that has a significant positive effect on the outcome – however, it is not robust across all models.

Figures 3 and 4 show the coefficient plots for the implementation of police reform and the regulations of paramilitary groups, respectively. Since the coefficient plots cross the 0 line in both cases, there is no predicted relationship. Only previous experiences of democracy is relevant for the survival of peace.

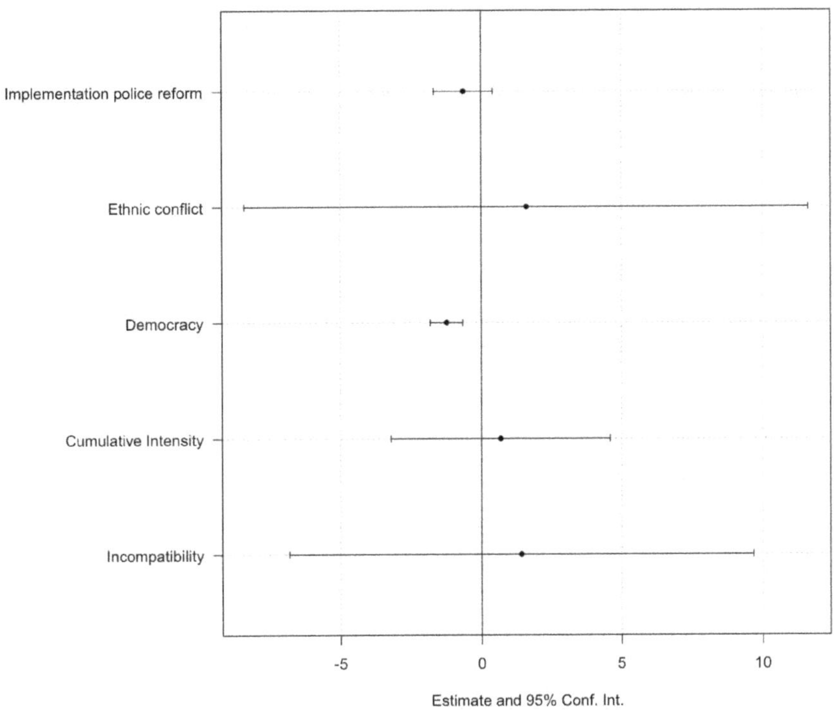

Figure 3 Coefficient plot on implementation of police reform

The findings point to two important aspects when it comes to SSR in post-war countries that directly relate to our theoretical framework. First, the inclusion of provisions on SSR is important when it comes to the establishment of lasting peace in post-war societies. As indicated by previous research (e.g., Walter 2002), credible commitments such as provisions in peace agreements are important to get the conflict parties to the table and to get them to agree to a peace agreement. However, our analysis also shows that the results are less clear when it comes to the implementation of provisions and their correlation with the survival of peace.

The data show that a commitment to SSR is pivotal for the establishment of peace in the aftermath of war, which is in line with our theoretical framework. This is particularly telling for the interests of the warring parties, who are usually the signatories of the peace agreements – they are the ones who want to see this issue area included in the peace agreements. This commitment to SSR during the negotiations provides a crucial turning point for the end of the war and the beginning of a peace period. At the same time, the data also show that the implementation of these reform promises is not as straightforward as one might expect; as we will see in our case studies, this often comes with a lot of difficulties

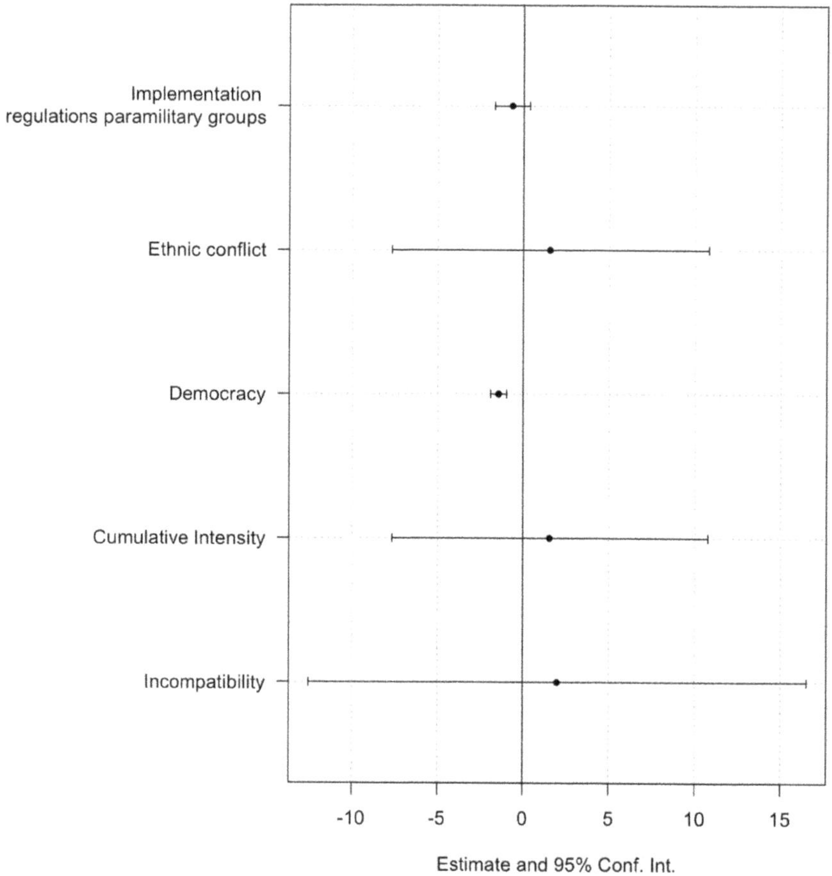

Figure 4 Coefficient plot on reform and regulation of paramilitary groups

and is inhibited by violent dynamics in the society. Quantitative data on gender or ethnic minorities as part of SSR continues to be limited, especially when it comes to post-war countries. This is one caveat of our statistical analysis, which is why we complement it with a qualitative analysis of two specific cases. Even if the implementation of SSR is fraught with problems, our case studies evidence that engaging in SSR continues to be the best options, as it brings together different societal actors and initiates a process of change that otherwise would not be there, risking a renewed recurrence of violence. While our quantitative data might not show positive support for a correlation between the implementation of SSR and peace, they also do not indicate a negative correlation. This means that even in a worst-case scenario, it does not necessarily contribute to a renewal of violence.

We also analysed the effect of justice sector provisions on the survival of peace, particularly with the help of the JSGR dataset. The first thing to note is that there are a lot of variables in the dataset, such as on the integration of women or ethnic minorities, or representation of regional groups, in the justice sector that are important for our theoretical frame but where there is no information either due to a lack of reform measures or available data in post-war countries. The justice sector is often treated as an afterthought in post-war countries, so any kinds of reforms take place only many years, if not decades, after the war has ended.

A few variables are important when looking at justice sector provisions and the survival of peace. Table 3 presents the result of the survival analysis with the recurrence of violent armed conflict as a dependent variable, whereas

Table 3 Survival analysis and war recurrence

	Model 1
Amnesty law	-0.596**
	(0.214)
Peace agreement	-1.642***
	(0.265)
Complaint mechanisms	-1.604***
	(0.410)
General impunity	1.528***
	(0.224)
Reform gender representation judiciary	0.491
	(0.306)
Reform ethnic representation judiciary	-0.151
	(0.595)
Traditional justice mechanisms	0.278
	(0.277)
Ethnic conflict	-0.186
	(0.258)
Democracy	-0.510+
	(0.275)
UN peacekeeping force	0.970***
	(0.233)
Incompatibility	-0.647**
	(0.236)
Num.Obs.	398
AIC	1337.4
BIC	1381.2
RMSE	0.52

+ $p < 0.1$, * $p < 0.05$, ** $p < 0.01$, *** $p < 0.001$

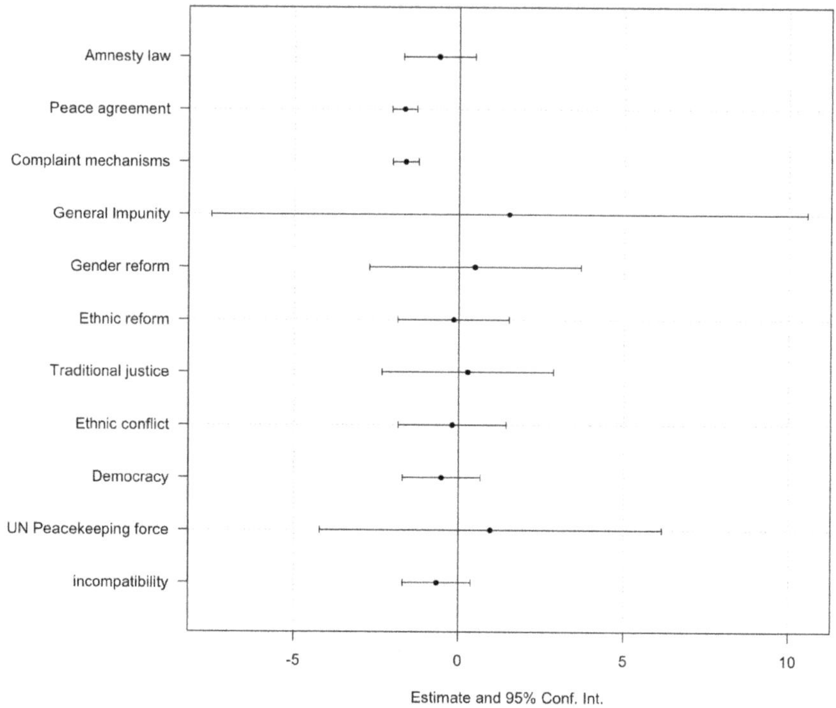

Figure 5 Coefficient plot on justice sector provisions

Figure 5 presents the coefficient plot of the relevant data. In particular, the existence of a peace agreement is – perhaps unsurprisingly – correlated with the survival of peace. Likewise, if there are complaint mechanisms on the justice sector, and if they are well known, we can also see a correlation with the establishment of post-war peace. Other justice sector variables, such as reform on gender components of the judiciary, or the existence of traditional justice mechanisms, are not correlated with post-war peace. While the table shows that variables such as the existence of an amnesty law, general impunity, UN peacekeeping force, or incompatibility are significant, the coefficient plot does not indicate a relationship with the survival of peace.

The evidence again underlines the importance of a commitment towards a written agreement as an important cornerstone on the pathway to peace. From the judiciary data presented here, most of the variables do not show a significant correlation with post-war peace. The correlation with complaint mechanisms shows how important the transparency and availability of institutional frameworks are for post-war societies, particularly when it comes to human and civil rights, and especially for women and ethnic minorities.

As outlined in our conceptual discussion earlier, there are some caveats to quantitative analysis. In particular, peace is more than just the absence of organized, collective violence (armed conflict or war) measured at a certain point in time; rather, it is a holistic process that includes other aspects of society. Therefore, this quantitative analysis is just a first step that will be complemented by a qualitative comparative analysis of two representative cases from different areas.

5 Comparative Case Studies: A Societal Perspective on Security Sector Reform in Afghanistan and Colombia

In this section, we provide a structured comparison of the SSR process from the perspective of our guiding question, which is how SSR can contribute to constructive and inclusive state–society relations and build the path to long-lasting peace. We selected two countries – Afghanistan and Colombia – that seem very different in those context conditions important for SSR (Sedra 2017, 103–56) such as political regime, civil society, and external intervention in SSR. With the help of these cross-regional case studies, we are able to show how functional equivalents of state institutions can contribute to peacebuilding in particular in areas where statehood is limited. At the same time, we argue that the adherence to basic human rights and the inclusion of gender and minority perspectives are fundamentally important to avoid the creation of an authoritarian peace, or peace that is merely the absence of war but retains other manifestations of violence.

We aim to show similarities and differences of SSR cross-regionally, and the impact on the outcome of peace. Two cases are of particular relevance here, while others are consulted as illustrative evidence. First, we examine state–society relations in Colombia, where violent disputes between societal groups and governments over power and control in the country have dominated the political, economic, and social landscape for the last five decades. Starting in the 1980s, policies of peacebuilding varied between reforming the state and its institutions (e.g., via decentralization and democratization policies) and strengthening the Colombian state and its military capabilities. Particularly in the last 30 years, there has been a shift towards a greater leadership of civil society actors in the reform process. At the end of the 1980s, the quest for a new constitution was mainly driven by student activists and some reformers in the traditional party system. The new constitution from 1991 has a strong emphasis on human rights and citizenship and is the first in Latin America to recognize the role of indigenous customary law (Uprimny 2014) as a complement to the formal judiciary. It took traditional elites a while to recognize the new constitution's transformative power. Since the mid-1990s, Colombia has seen a strong element of outside security intervention in the form of military aid by the United States to the Pastrana and Uribe governments (1998–2002 and 2002–2010, respectively). While the main goal of Plan Colombia was to combat drug production and trade, the line between anti-drug and counterinsurgency policies was always blurred. Since the 1990s, the demobilization of some armed groups (Movimiento 19 de Abril (M-19), parts of the Ejército de Liberación Nacional (ELN)) and the legal frame of the new constitution led to the establishment of NGOs that had a crucial role later in the monitoring of the demobilization of paramilitary groups; this led to the revelation of the close links among right-wing parliamentarians, paramilitaries, and drug organizations (so-called 'para-politics'). The peace agreement between the government of Juan Manuel Santos (2010–2018) and the FARC-EP signed in 2016 included a process of DDR for the FARC-EP combatants, but reform of the state security forces was taboo until recently. The very repressive strategies of the Colombian police during the massive protests in the last three years have increased calls by civil society for profound police reform. Various attempts and initiatives to reform the police have been triggered by excessive police brutality or corruption (1993, 2003, 2021). Current pressure by civil society led the government of Iván Duque (2018–2022) to introduce its own (albeit extremely limited) reform plans, emphasizing oversight and introducing new uniforms. The new government, which came into power in 2022, presented much more ambitious reform plans such as unhinging the police from the Defence Ministry and the latter's inclusion into a new Ministry of Peace, Security, and Conviviality. While past reforms have been accompanied by conflict and violence, Colombia serves as a case study for the room for manoeuvre for civil society through human rights guarantees in the constitution and their active role in advocating for SSR. In this case study, we look holistically at the societal dynamics of the peacebuilding process, and what roles non-state actors can play alongside state and external actors in the reform of the security sector.

While Colombia claims to be the oldest democracy in Latin America, violence has been a permanent pattern of its political and social context. A diversity of non-state armed actors have been present since the mid-twentieth century, such as traditional leftist guerrilla groups, right-wing paramilitary groups, and criminal organizations (Berquist, Peñaranda, and Sánchez 2001; Richani 2002; González González 2014). Regarding SSR, Colombia had a series of DDR processes prior to the peace agreement signed with the FARC-EP in 2016. Most of these agreements were processes of demobilization and demilitarization and did not have a broader scope. The 2016 agreement is comprehensive, including some structural reforms (regarding land), strategies to tackle drug production, and a special gender focus. However, it is also a rare example of a peace accord that does not mention police and military reform. Taking a longer view on institutional reforms, Colombia is special regarding the timing of a profound reform of the judiciary, which had already taken place in 1991.

We also analyse the most recent example of Afghanistan as a process that was heavily driven by outside forces and is not embedded in its historical, cultural, and economic context. Security sector reform in Afghanistan prioritized government interests over local concerns, which makes it a fitting case study to explore the effect of SSR that is not situated in a wider societal context on the pathway to peace, as we hypothesize in our theoretical framework.

Afghanistan is home to a variety of non-state armed actors but has historically also been the playground for international interventions by a variety of actors such as the British Empire, the Soviet Union, and the United States and NATO. At the level of the central state, the country has experienced a variety of regimes, such as an Islamic regime after 1992 and the Taliban takeover between 1996 and 2001, followed by a fragile democratization under the tutelage of the United States and NATO after 2001 (Giustozzi 2019; Dearing 2022). The G8 donor countries supported substantial reforms to the security sector, designating lead donors for specific sectors with not always compatible agendas (such as police reform, where Germany was the lead nation but the United States the most important donor) and a significant lack of local ownership. Security sector reform was only superficially mentioned in the Bonn Agreement of 2002, and was later driven by increasing violence (Sedra 2017, 2018). The withdrawal of the United States and other foreign troops in 2021 linked to the return to power of the Taliban turned Afghanistan into a showcase for the failure of externally driven SSR and peacebuilding strategies. This was unsurprising given that numerous experts had warned that the reforms lacked local ownership and were not sustainable in political and financial terms (Goodhand 2009; Giustozzi 2012a; Sedra 2017).

Afghanistan and Colombia share structural similarities regarding the level and duration of violence and armed conflict, as this refers to battle-related deaths, extrajudicial killings, and violent displacement, which were ongoing throughout SSR and shaped the respective policy approaches towards violence (Table 4). At the same time, both countries show high levels of subnational variation regarding the provision of security and justice, where the central state is just one of the actors (and often not the most important one), as well as a historic lack of a state monopoly of force. Finally, both countries suffer from the existence of war economy structures financing armed actors through the production and trade of illicit drugs (opium and coca crops) with transborder, transregional, and international trade networks.

Table 4 Timeline of SSR and peacebuilding in Afghanistan and Colombia since 1989

	Afghanistan	**Colombia**
1989	Peace agreement and withdrawal of the Soviet troops, very fragile communist regime	
1990		Peace process and demobilization of M-19 and other smaller guerrilla groups
1991		New constitution
1992	Mujaheddin, other armed groups and warlords storm the capital and form an Islamic government	
1995	Taliban take over	
1998–9		Failed peace process (Caguán) between the government and the FARC-EP → increase in violence
2000		Plan Colombia
2001	Taliban ousted by international coalition and Northern Alliance	
2002	Loya Jirga in Bonn, Germany → Karzai elected interim president until elections in 2004 Donor conference on military reform → Afghan National Army built from scratch → Agreement on police reform between the Afghan Ministry of the Interior and the German government	Start of demobilization process of paramilitary groups (until 2006)

2004	Loya Jirga adopts new constitution (input of 500,000 Afghans)	
2005	Stakeholder conference Justice for All (rejected by donors as too ambitious in 2007)	
	First elections in more than 30 years	
2010	NATO announces military retreat	
2012		Start of dialogue between the Colombian government and the FARC-EP in Havana
2014	NATO combat mission ends, but is on and off due to increasing levels of violence	
2016		Peace agreement signed but referendum failed
2021	Taliban oust the elected government and take over	
2022		Gustavo Petro elected as the first leftist president promoting a profound reform of the security sector

Our perspective on state–society relations regarding comprehensive SSR will analyse the four parts of SSR (DDR, police, military, and judicial reform) emphasizing the elements highlighted in our conceptual frame: the inclusion of society, and specifically women and ethnic minorities; the importance of human rights and violence reduction; the existence and inclusion of functional equivalents into the reform process, and the role of external actors.

5.1 Disarmament, Demobilization, and Reintegration: (No) Role for Civil Society?

In our theoretical frame, we formulated that in order for a state–society perspective on DDR to contribute to peace in a society, it must include an analysis of the whole range of non-state armed actors, the relations between armed actors and society, and the relations in and with the communities that reintegrate former combatants. Other important questions are related to overcoming ex-combatants' stigmatization and/or marginalization, in addition to patterns of economic and social inclusion that disincentivize the taking up of arms again. Finally, the transformation of war-time bonds into constructive processes of building social cohesion is also of great importance in post-war SSR.

Over the last two decades, both Afghanistan and Colombia experienced a number of processes aiming at the demobilization, demilitarization, and (re-)integration of non-state armed actors. Both countries see a variety of non-state armed actors operating in their territories, including rebels such as the Colombian guerrilla groups, or the Afghan Mujaheddin, militias, paramilitary groups, and drug organizations. Some of these groups are highly embedded in local power structures (e.g., Afghan local militias, warlords, or Colombian rebels in some places), while others have power due to their violent control of some territories. Nevertheless, the main difference between both countries is related to (a) the military situation and the patterns of war termination shaping the conditions of DDR; (b) different attitudes of civil society regarding demobilized actors; and (c) dissimilar levels and patterns of foreign engagement.

Colombia has a long tradition of disarming non-state armed actors, mostly via agreements and amnesties. During a variety of peace process, the demobilization of armed groups was initiated, starting with the Betancur administration (1982–1986). In 1985, FARC members and ex-combatants established the Unión Patriótica (UP), a leftist political party, but over 3,000 representatives, members, and candidates were murdered during the subsequent years (Melo Moreno and Centro de Memoria Histórica (Colombia) 2018). Between 1988 and 1991 talks between the government and eight guerrilla groups, including the M-19 and a splinter group of the ELN, Corriente de Renovación Socialista, demobilized 4,715 fighters. Again, protection and security for those demobilized was a major problem. Carlos Pizarro Leongómez, the leader of M-19 who had signed the peace agreement and was the M-19's presidential candidate, was assassinated in April 1990, as had been two other presidential candidates, Bernardo Jaramillo of the UP in March 1990, and Luis Carlos Galán, the founder of Nuevo Liberalismo (New Liberalism), a splinter of the Liberal Party, in August 1989. Direct responsibility for these assassinations remains unclear but can be attributed to so-called sicarios or hitmen paid by large landowners, right-wing elites, organized crime, or others resisting any reform.

The 1990s saw an increase in violence in the context of the expansion of drug production and trafficking, a failed peace process between the government and the FARC-EP, and in 2002 the election of a rather authoritarian government under Álvaro Uribe (2002–2010). In the shadow of the attacks of 9/11, Uribe framed the guerrilla as narco-terrorists with whom negotiations were not possible. The only demobilization initiatives his government pursued were related to the paramilitary forces that considered themselves as a state-substitute in fighting the guerrilla groups (Romero 2003). As Figures 6 and 7 show, more than 70,000 members of armed groups demobilized – most of them individually – and 13,000 FARC-EP fighters demobilized collectively after the signing of the peace agreement in 2016. The demobilization of the paramilitary groups was highly controversial because Uribe did not establish major conditions for demobilizing. Only after massive protests by national and international human rights organizations did the United Nations, and some European governments amend the legal basis (initially slightly), which was later revised by the

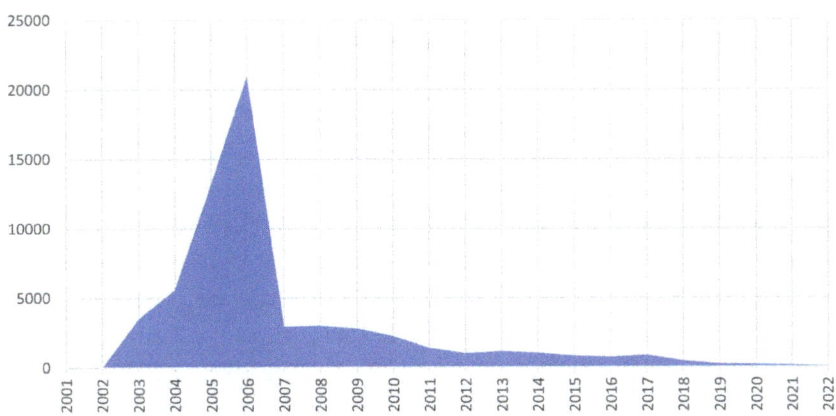

Figure 6 Colombia: Individual demobilization 2001–2021

Source: Author's elaboration based on www.datos.gov.co/Inclusion-Social-y-Reconciliacion/Historico-de-personas-desmovilizadas/uea5-is6n/data

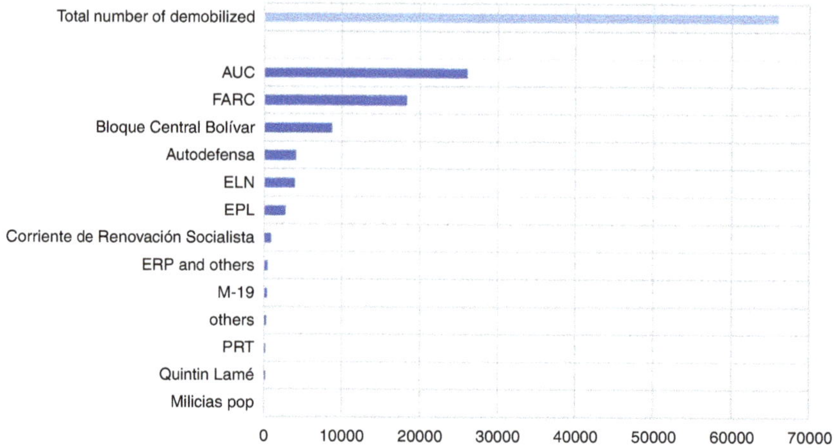

Figure 7 Colombia: Demobilized combatants per non-state armed group 2001–2020

Source: Author's elaboration based on www.datos.gov.co/Justicia-y-Derecho/Desmovilizaciones-por-grupo-armado/wavk-2hmm

Colombian Supreme Court to adhere to a minimum standard of accountability such as regarding truth telling (Gutiérrez Sanín and González Peña 2012). Human rights advocacy by international and national actors was necessary even though Colombia had signed the Rome Statute of the International Criminal Court in 2002, as it had excluded war crimes for a period of 7 years after signing.

In Afghanistan, the United States armed forces and allied Afghan armed groups of the Northern Alliance killed between 8,000 and 12,000 members of the Taliban in 2001, ousting them from Kabul and witnessing their leader and others flee to Pakistan (Giustozzi 2019, 18). From 2003 to 2006 under the lead of the Japanese government, the DDR process implemented by UNDP targeted former members of the Afghan Military Forces and of non-state militias to encourage their transition into civilian life (Hartzell 2011; Figure 8). As part of the DDR programme, 63,000 non-state armed actors were disarmed and demobilized between 2003 and 2005 by the United Nations. The follow-up programme DIAG (Disbandment of Illegal Armed Groups) between 2006 and 2011 was led by the Afghan government and targeted the members of those more than 2,000 militias operating outside of Kabul and beyond the control of the central state. However, as the Taliban began to reorganize and violence increased in the context of the 2005 elections, external actors did little to enforce demobilization of local militias, instead trying to include them in counterinsurgency (Derksen 2015). A significant number of former combatants were included into the newly established police forces and the Afghan National Army (ANA), although the official agreement was that they should not

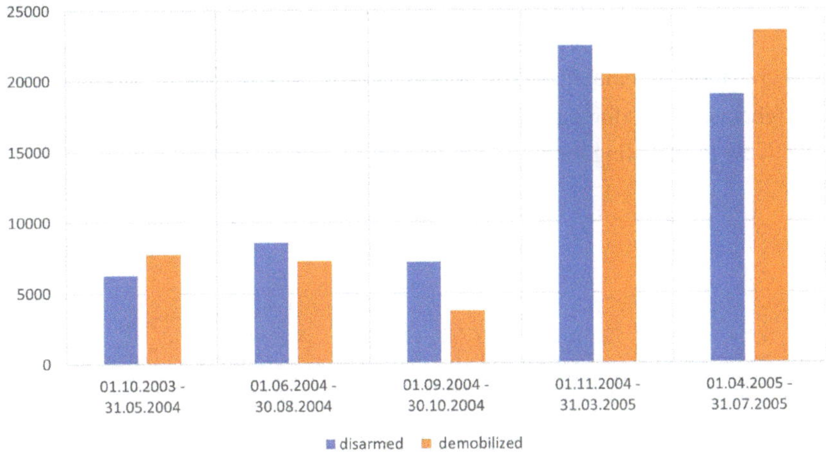

Figure 8 Afghanistan: Disarmed and demobilized 2003–2005

Source: Authors representation based on UN data cited in (Hartzell 2011, 5)

exceed 10–20 per cent. As Giustozzi (2012a, 62) observed, there were significant levels of rearmament leading to an 'unofficial compromise on disarmament and demobilization, involving the establishment of a facade process of disarmament, behind which non-state armed groups of various types would be allowed to continue to exist and sometimes prosper, as long as they were willing to pay at least lip service to the bureaucratic process and abstained from actively working against the government in charge'. Disarmament and demobilization in Afghanistan were only done half-heartedly, and combatants were often integrated into the existing security forces. Instead of a thorough demobilization of forces, this led to a perpetuation of the war logic in new structures.

Summarizing and comparing the experiences during the various DDR processes we can observe the following similarities.

Disarmament, demobilization, and reintegration included some non-state armed actors, but not all. The processes between these groups were different. In Colombia, for example, the guerrilla groups received full amnesty for laying down arms during the 1990s, but paramilitaries and the FARC-EP were submitted to transitional justice mechanisms, had to help clarify what they had done, and received reduced sentences. In Afghanistan, however, no such mechanisms were established. Taliban dispersed into the peripheral rural areas or across the border and other groups such as militias were privy to some reintegration packages including financial support, alphabetization, and vocational training. This points to the importance of the societal context in the process, as outlined in our theoretical framework. In Colombia, we can at least see an attempt at societal integration of former fighters, whereas this was not the case in Afghanistan.

In Colombia, there was a significant drop in violence after the process with the AUC (Figure 9); however, similar to Afghanistan (Figure 10), success was limited as fighters remobilized or joined other groups. The growing security crisis in Afghanistan 'reinforced communities' reliance on militias to provide safety, effectively legitimating the role of militia commanders' (Hartzell 2011, 9)

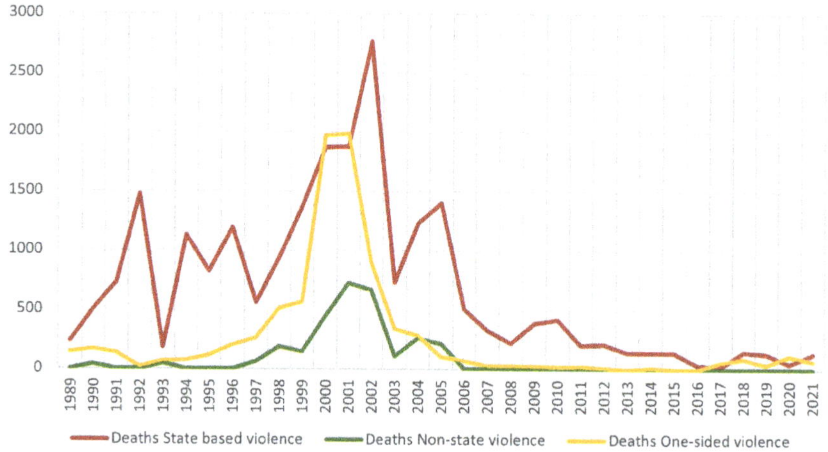

Figure 9 Colombia: Violence 1989–2021

Source: Author's elaboration based on Uppsala Conflict Data Program (UCDP) https://ucdp.uu.se/country/100

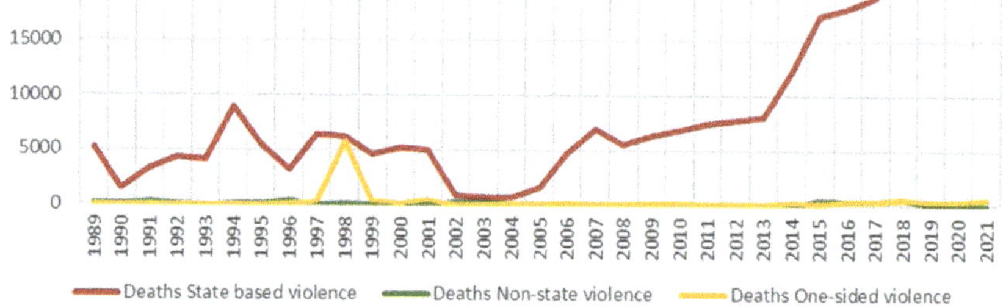

Figure 10 Afghanistan: Violence 1989–2021

Source: Author's elaboration based on Uppsala Conflict Data Program (UCDP) https://ucdp.uu.se/country/700

Stigmatization and/or marginalization was not directed against demobilized ex-combatants in either country, but as the process did not include all non-state armed actors, both governments declared the remaining groups illegal, criminal actors. In Afghanistan, demobilized combatants were either integrated into the new armed forces and police forces or simply stayed at home in their communities. Caroline Hartzell (2011, 5) observed: 'Between the war's end and the program's initiation, many AMF [Afghan Military Forces] combatants had become part-time soldiers and officers with family homes and strong ties to their local communities'. The process was somewhat different in Colombia due to the legal conditions of truth telling for reduced sentences under the Law of Peace and Justice (No. 975, 2005). Nevertheless, many paramilitaries were able to hold onto their violently acquired land and other resources, many thousands returned to combat, and the enabling structures stayed intact (Gutiérrez Sanín and González Peña 2012, 114–6). After the peace accord of 2016 the main difference was that FARC-EP combatants could demobilize collectively in so-called ETCR (Espacios Territoriales de Capacitación y Reintegración, Territorial Spaces for Capacitation and Reintegration). Experiences in these territories vary. Comparing different experiences, Romero (2021, 123) noted:

> reintegration is a complex issue that requires coordination and leadership between and within the state, ex-combatants, and society. This has been in short supply, especially during the Duque government, elected by a coalition of forces largely opposed to peace negotiations and the Agreement. In other words, a favourable political context is key for the success of reintegration and peacebuilding processes.

However, again, ex-combatants were obliged to contribute to truth finding and to appear before the Special Judiciary for Peace, which investigated some major cases of gross human rights violations such as kidnapping.

Analysing these experiences under our state-society perspective, we can clearly see that they did not overcome the main deficits of mainstream DDR. The processes did not include non-state armed groups that did not sign a peace agreement; except for the DDR process with the FARC-EP, they focused on individual fighters and not on community building and, maybe most importantly, they did not provide civilian livelihoods to disincentivize taking up arms again.

5.2 Reforming the Armed Forces and the Police under the Logic of Counterinsurgency

While we have observed a series of similarities in the DDR processes of each country, reform of the state's security institutions (armed forces and police) has looked very different. In Afghanistan, external actors established new institutions from scratch, even though a significant number of demobilized combatants from the anti-Taliban forces were admitted into these institutions. The USA took the lead regarding the armed forces, while Germany led the reform of the police. Reforms in Colombia aimed to strengthen the efficacy and increase the numerical strength of the existing institution. While external influence was limited compared to Afghanistan, the US-sponsored Plan Colombia stood at the core. Here, fighting drug production (and insurgency) were the main unaccomplished goals (GAO (US Government Accountability Office 2008). The Colombian police have been part of the Defence Ministry since the 1950s. The underlying rationale was to depoliticize the police after a decade of civil war between the main political parties.

In our theoretical chapter, we claimed that a state–society approach to the reform of the armed forces and the police must complement the traditional emphasis on mandate, oversight, and efficiency with an analysis of the mobilization and social recruitment strategies. From this perspective, the countries show similarities as mobilization and recruitment followed political criteria. In Afghanistan (Sedra 2017, 172–88), a decree establishing the new ANA composed of 70,000 troops was issued in 2002 following the donor's conference in Bonn, Germany. This process was heavily driven by rising insecurity due to the reorganization of the Taliban. Despite the introduction of an ethnic quota system in 2003, there was a huge imbalance: Hartzell (2011, 9) cited 'data from an Afghan official in January 2010 [who] finds that Pashtuns represented 42.6 percent of the army, Tajiks 40.98 percent, Hazaras 7.68 percent, Uzbeks 4.05 percent, and other minorities 4.68 percent, and concludes that while the presence of Pashtuns at all levels of the military corresponds to their proportion of the general population, Tajiks continue to dominate the officer and non-commissioned officer ranks'. This imbalance reflects the country's fragmentation and the – often violent – conflicts around attempts to centralize military power.

Like Afghanistan, the Colombian state never had a monopoly on force in the country and reforms were mostly a function of counterinsurgency policies. After the failure of the peace process under the Pastrana administration (1998–2002), reforms were 'limited' (Grabendorff 2009) in the sense that their aim was to increase the capacities and the territorial control of the state, but not engender a fundamental transformation of the society. Therefore, within South America, Colombia's armed forces are second only to Brazil's in terms of member numbers. The main mandate of Colombia's armed forces was to fight the 'internal enemy' – that is, the armed guerrilla groups FARC-EP and ELN, while cooperating at least implicitly with the paramilitary groups. Nevertheless, the peace agreement of 2016 does not include any provisions on institutional reforms in the state security sector such as the separation of internal and external mandates between the military and the police or the establishment of a civilian police force. The peace agreement mentions only the military and the police in relation to some monitoring functions of the FARC-EP's DDR process.

Recruiting strategies for the police in Afghanistan after 2002 produced a similar ethnic imbalance as manifested in the ANA, although there was no reform from scratch but a strategy of transforming the existing institution. A National Police Academy was established that trained officers but not ordinary ranks. The police are the most visible state institution for citizens. However, in rural areas of Afghanistan, traditional providers of security serve as functional equivalents in the absence of the state. The somewhat transformed national police are present mostly in the larger urban areas. Sedra (2017, 185) cited a survey from 2014 where the police and the judiciary were considered the most corrupt institutions in the country. Involvement in drug trafficking seems to be a major contributing factor to that attitude.

At the same time, gender was a major element of police reform supported extensively by the European Union through the EUPOL Afghanistan mission. The more active participation of women in the security sector was a priority at the outset of the international mission since there was a lack of gender representation across the board (Ansorg and Haastrup 2018, 1136). Thus, gender was inscribed into the design and conceptualization of the mission. While EUPOL achieved some gains, such as by helping the Afghan government establish Family Response Units within the ANP, the inclusion of women in the police force progressed very slowly. An audit conducted 7 years after the mission found that women comprised only 2 per cent of the new police force (European Court of Auditors 2015). Since the withdrawal of the international forces and the renewed takeover by the Taliban regime, the achievements of the mission with regard to gender mainstreaming have been reversed. Despite heavy international engagement over two decades, prevalent societal norms were reinforced almost overnight.

Colombia's police are part of the armed forces and have been involved in the counterinsurgency and counternarcotics strategies. Nevertheless, certain reforms have been initiated, such as the increasing inclusion of women into the police at all levels. In 2021, over 14 per cent of the police force were female (Policía Nacional de Colombia, Bogotá DC, Colombia et al. 2021). However, a series of anti-government protests in 2019 and 2021 provided evidence for the highly repressive police approaches and a lack of constructive police–community relations (Nilsson and Jonsson 2022). These events increased advocacy in civil society organizations for a profound reform of the police (Grupo de Trabajo FIP – FESCOL 2021). Separating the police from the military and making it a civilian force providing public security is one of the main demands

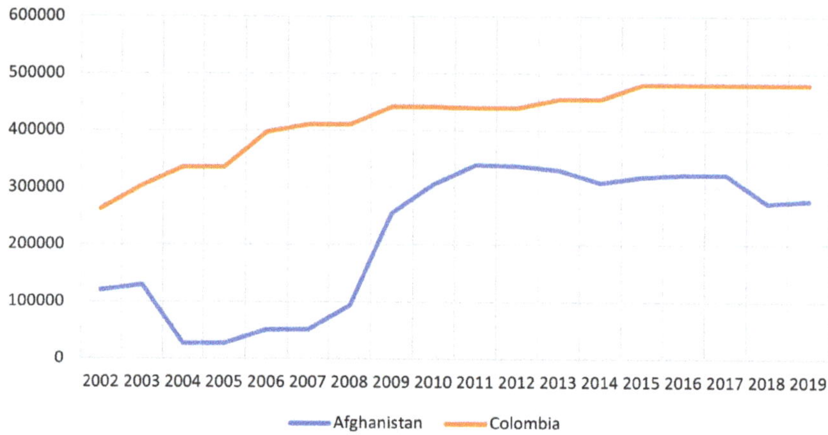

Figure 11 Increase of military manpower in Colombia and Afghanistan (2002–2019)

Source: Author's elaboration based on World Bank based on IISS Military Balance https://data.worldbank.org/indicator/MS.MIL.TOTL.P1?end=2019&name_desc=false&start=2000

of civil society and a central reform project of the progressive government elected in 2022.

In both Colombia and Afghanistan, the dominance of counterinsurgency in security policies has proved highly problematic, particularly when it comes to everyday relations among the military, the police, and the respective society. This is most visible in the militarization of public security (Figure 11) as well as the lack of accountability and gross violations of human rights by state security institutions. The persistence of illegal, criminal economies, most notably (but not exclusively) in the production and trade in opium (Afghanistan) and coca (Colombia), has also contributed to violence and corruption in both countries. At the same time, international and national strategies have promoted militarization and repression.

In Afghanistan, the rising Taliban insurgency and the increased role of the USA in training and financing led to the police becoming increasingly militarized, which often went hand in hand with gross human rights violations. The documentation of human rights violations in Afghanistan usually focuses on the Taliban's current and past attacks on women and those opposing either their own views or those of local militias (Human Rights Watch 2005; Gossman and Kline 2015). However, the new and transformed Afghan military and police also committed human rights violations and are highly corrupt, as shown by the admittedly scant research (Singh 2014) and reports by international NGOs such as Human Rights Watch (Reid and Muhammedally 2011).

Over the last two decades in Colombia, civil society organizations at the national and local level have denounced a variety of gross human rights violations committed by the armed forces and by the police. The most prominent case are the extrajudicial killings, the so-called false positives (*falsos positivos*). Between 2002 and 2008, the military assassinated over 6,000 young men from poor marginalized neighbourhoods, put them in clothes resembling guerrilla uniforms, and claimed that they were guerrilleros who had died in combat. The Commission for the Clarification of Truth, Coexistence and Non-Repetition (Truth Commission) tells a very different story in its report (Comisión para el Esclarecimiento de la Verdad, la Convivencia y la No Repetición 2022, 757): 'The "false positives" were committed on the basis of decisions embodied in regulations issued through institutional channels in the form of laws, decrees, ministerial directives, circulars and directives issued by the security forces that led to extrajudicial executions.' Other patterns of gross human rights violations include forced displacement, mostly by paramilitary groups but often in at least implicit cooperation with the military and regional elites (Tellez 2021). After the signature of the peace agreement, there was increased violence against demobilized former combatants, human rights defenders, and social leaders.

Military and police reform in both countries did not take into account a holistic, societal perspective that focuses on communities and the link between security and the wider civil society as outlined in our theoretical framework. Instead, reforms were targeted at counterinsurgency measures in the light of ongoing violence. In Colombia, the police continue to be part of the armed forces and contribute to the militarization of society. Gross human rights violations, especially against innocent men who were framed as guerrillas, were part of the harsh counterinsurgency measures in the country. Likewise, in Afghanistan, society was characterized by ongoing violence and the attempt to counter this with strict military measures. While the police in Afghanistan are separate from the military, both security institutions were highly militarized and served the fight against insurgency rather than the creation of safety and order in local communities.

Functional equivalents to the state provision of security play a major role in both countries. In Afghanistan, local militias maintain control and order in remote rural areas and these have even been supported or created by the US forces due to the deteriorating security situation (Felbab-Brown 2016). In Colombia, these equivalents are non-state armed groups of various backgrounds such as the remaining guerrilla ELN or FARC-EP dissidents, as well as different groups active in the criminal economy. Indigenous or Afro-Colombian guards at the community level are the only ones with a legal recognition. In rural areas where indigenous or Afro-Colombian communities dominate, they can serve as a form of non-violent self-protection (Chaves, Aarts, and van Bommel 2020). They complement, rather than replace, state security forces. Along the lines of our theoretical framework, we thus conclude that they are an important security actor in the country. In both countries, the governments largely failed to develop a systematic policy regarding these non-state armed forces. The current initiative of the Colombian government (Total Peace) to demobilize all non-state armed groups, either via negotiations or via the submission under the law, is an interesting innovation whose results remain to be seen.

5.3 Transitional Justice and Judicial Reform: Centrepiece or Afterthought?

The role of transitional justice and judicial reform in terms of timing, content, and depth are the main differences shaping SSR in Colombia and Afghanistan. The latter resembles the experience of many post-war societies where judicial reform comes last, if at all (see Section 4). Civil society initiatives to cope with past human rights violations and hold perpetrators accountable were quite successful in Colombia, but in Afghanistan have been side-lined by political elites and international actors.

Three interrelated problems stand out with regard to transitional justice and judicial reform in Afghanistan: First, international actors prioritized 'hard security' over justice, disregarded existing institutions, and attempted to rationalize the legal framework shaped by the overlapping of state, sharia, and customary law in the 2004 constitution. This limited service provision in the judicial sector and generated conflicts around the legal framework – such as the criminal process code – not just between international and local actors but even among the international donors (Sedra 2017, 190–204). Second, the Bonn Agreement delegated transitional justice to the newly created Human Rights Commission (Rubin 2003). However, this body lacked international support and therefore leverage. For example, the former commissioner on transitional justice of the Afghanistan Independent Human Rights Commission, Ahmed Nader Nadery (2007), criticized the international community for its lack of interest in victims' rights, arguing that the promotion of a strategy of 'peace first, justice later' led to more violence and impunity. Third, state institutions in the justice sector are highly corrupt (Singh 2014). Sedra (2017, 202) cited an UNODC report from 2010 in which it is estimated that 23 per cent of Afghanistan's GDP was spent on bribes, mostly to the police and the justice sector.

In Colombia, by contrast, a new constitution (1991) and strengthening the independence of the judiciary in securing human rights were present at the outset of a series of peace negotiations with various non-state armed groups.

The new legal frame and its emphasis on the protection of human rights empowered civil society and non-violent advocacy for change and reforms (Nielson and Shugart 1999; Uprimny 2003; Kurtenbach 2017b). The peace agreement of 2016 with the FARC-EP increased the scope of action, as political opposition could no longer be framed in terms of the internal war. Transitional justice mechanisms and the prioritization of victims' rights started even before the peace agreements. In 2011, the Colombian Congress approved Law 1448 (the Victims Law, establishing, amongst other things, the National Victims Register). While there are high levels of violence against human rights defenders, social leaders, and demobilized combatants (INDEPAZ 2020), Law 1448 has proven highly important for the involvement of society in post-war reforms. In 2022, the Colombian Truth Commission presented a comprehensive report and formulated important recommendations such as the profound reform of the armed forces and the police (Comisión para el Esclarecimiento de la Verdad, la Convivencia y la No Repetición 2022). Implementation will be key.

Our theoretical framework emphasizes that broader policies of human rights promotion and judicial reforms beyond transitional justice mechanisms are key for state–society relations. Our quantitative analysis and our case studies both provide evidence for this claim. Colombia is a rare case of a profound constitutional and judicial reform paving the way for non-violent advocacy of human rights in a variety of contexts (victims, minorities, women, etc.) as a basis for highly contested change.

6 State–Society Relations and the Establishment of Peace

Security sector reform is and will remain a key element of peacebuilding, as the reduction of violence is a main aim across all societies, independent of the specific approaches to doing so. Our focus on state–society relations and our empirical results not only provide an innovative conceptual approach emphasizing the importance of human rights, but also have important implications for SSR policies on the ground and avenues for future research.

6.1 Security Sector Reform in State–Society Relations

The joint findings of our quantitative and qualitative analysis provide evidence on the importance of a state–society perspective on SSR related to four elements.

First, the inclusion of all armed actors in processes of DDR is important for the establishment of peace in post-war societies. Our quantitative analysis shows the importance of including paramilitary actors, including militias and mercenaries, for the survival of peace. Accords such as those in Sierra Leone, Macedonia, and Guatemala included provisions on the regulation of paramilitary groups, and the post-war process also saw the implementation of such provisions. In Sierra Leone, for example, the thorough input of local actors in SSR through a comprehensive consultation process put the implementation of the reforms in line with societal needs and benefited the establishment of long-term peace (Onoma 2014). Findings from our qualitative case studies on Colombia and Afghanistan point in the same direction. The remobilization of combatants from only partially demobilized groups and their inclusion into either newly emerging or existing armed groups has been a major problem in both countries. This not only relates to a lack of provisions in peace agreements and their implementation, but also points toward a broader problem: the structural conditions that enable recruitment and mobilization of armed actors have not been targeted or changed in either Afghanistan or Colombia, or most other post-war contexts. War economies in the drug sector, as well as petty and organized crime, provide important sources of livelihood in the rural areas and thus help armed actors to survive and reorganize. The case of the Taliban is no exception here – examples of illicit resource extraction in the DR Congo or organized crime in the Sahel show that it is a common feature in (former) conflict regions. At the same time, the persistence of armed actors with or without political agendas puts pressure on the security institutions under reform. The reliance on well-established repressive and authoritarian answers undermines the pillars of reform, such as commitment to human rights and civilian control.

Second, our analysis shows that previous experience with democracy has a positive effect on the survival of peace. Our case studies provide evidence that the effect might not be related to democracy per se, but rather the strength of civil society to monitor reform processes, hold those in power accountable, and advocate for broader notions of peace, victim's rights, and human rights more generally. Our quantitative study shows that the accessibility and transparency of judicial complaints mechanisms makes a difference for the pathway to peace. Our qualitative comparison highlights the relevance of reforms towards an independent judiciary and the formal guarantee of human rights. As in peace agreements, the existence of a legal frame codifying human rights and opening civic space for civil societies is a pre-condition, and implementation is key. The Colombian experience provides important evidence for this. Other prominent cases evincing strong civil society engagement include Sierra Leone and Papua New Guinea.

Third, state institutions matter but not necessarily along the assumptions of mainstream policies. Our results show that the contribution of SSR to long-lasting peace does not rely on the strength of the military and the police. A focus on efficiency and military strength seems more related to the militarization of public security policies and the violation of human rights by the security institutions. Afghanistan and Colombia demonstrate how this undermines reform processes and de-legitimizes new (or existing) security institutions. Instead, successful peacebuilding seems to be related to the existence of an independent judiciary that is able to provide some justice to victims as well as protection and empowerment vis-à-vis non-armed actors, women, and marginalized ethnic groups. This is what human security is about: protection of public spaces to discuss and advocate for often conflicting approaches to politics, economy, and society without the use of violence. Likewise, these reform processes do not happen in the initial years after the war. The reform of the judiciary, including the involvement of underrepresented groups, and greater accountability of the judiciary, takes place only once other institutional areas, such as DDR, or reform of the police, have been established. However, this kind of sequencing delays the strengthening of state–society relations and, ultimately, the establishment of long-standing peace.

Last but not least, peace and security do not rely on the state and its institutions alone; they need to be complemented by other institutions serving as functional equivalents of state institutions. In post-war societies, international actors such as the International Court of Justice or peacekeeping missions play a major and often positive role, at least in the immediate aftermath of war termination. The unresolved problem is what happens when these missions leave. There are few examples of a successful and smooth transition in the medium and long term. The 'successful' cases of liberal peacebuilding in the early 1990s provide evidence of success in terms of minimalist peace (the non-recurrence of war) but also betray the existence of different patterns of violence or the emergence of new armed actors due to the lack of structural transformation. El Salvador is a paradigmatic case for the former development and Mozambique for the latter. Despite the debate on hybrid security, local institutions such as traditional authorities are still either disregarded or romanticized. These institutions can contribute to peace as long as they respect fundamental human rights and there is a clear framework around how and under what circumstances they complement state responsibilities. Again, Colombia is an interesting case, as the constitution of 1991 defined the complementary role of customary law early on.

6.2 Implications for Security Sector Reform Policies

Our quantitative and qualitative research, as well as other cases around the world (Ansorg and Kurtenbach 2022), show that one-size-fits-all approaches to SSR do not work in post-war countries. While security is considered a requirement for long-term peace, SSR is a highly context-specific and political endeavour that requires tailored solutions to complex post-war conditions. This should include specific attention to the inclusion of former rebel groups and other non-state armed actors; a holistic approach and linking of police to judiciary reform to provide public security for all citizens; recognition of the importance of non-state functional equivalents in the provision of security and justice under the condition of their adherence to basic human rights; and an increase in the representation of underrepresented groups such as particular ethnic groups or women. Afghanistan is the most obvious case providing evidence of that; others are the Democratic Republic of the Congo and Bosnia. Quantitative data show that most SSR efforts after the end of war are partial at best. While DDR programmes are state of the art and police reform plays a role, judicial reform and addressing issues with paramilitary and other non-state armed groups seem particularly hard to implement, even if assented to in peace agreements. This is often due to post-war power dynamics within the country, as the evidence from specific case studies shows. Thus, there is not one 'perfect' or even 'good' solution to the question of how to conduct SSR in a post-war country. Rather, it is about finding compromises for former warring parties and the broader population navigating the highly contested endeavour of peacebuilding in the shadow of war and mistrust.

Our analysis shows that despite all the difficulties in implementing SSR in the aftermath of war, it remains a pivotal aspect of the overall peacebuilding process: the commitment to reform enables warring actors to come to the negotiation table, agree to a settlement, and lay down their arms. This is an important first step in the peace process. While implementation of provisions is often deficient, our analysis, together with illustrative cases from other parts of the world, shows that it is still better than doing nothing altogether. The questions then are under what conditions it is more likely that the reform plans can be implemented, and how can the whole society be included in the process. A focus on human rights is key and despite often being contested, mostly by non-reform-oriented elites, should not be disregarded as a Western imposition. Individual and collective human rights are the main basis for citizens empowerment and participation in their communities and in broader society. Elites at the local and national levels see reforms as a zero-sum game and try to prevent a shift in power relations. The selective violence against human rights defenders, social representatives of community organizations, environmental activists, and independent journalists or judges across the globe is a common strategy of intimidation. The UN Special Rapporteur on Human Rights defenders observed 1,323 killings in 64 countries between 2015 and 2019 (Global Witness 2019; UN Special Rapporteur on Human Rights defenders, Mary Lawlor 2021). However, most cases remain without documentation and state institutions are either unable or unwilling to provide the necessary protection.

If the outcome of SSR is 'measured' in relation to a successful violence reduction, then state–society relations and the link between formal institutions and informal practices need to stand at the core of these activities. This has three practical consequences. First, the starting point of SSR needs to be political debate and broad coalitions involving all relevant societal stakeholders. The experiences of the United Nations War-Torn Societies Project in Guatemala show how important this is (Torres-Rivas and Arévalo de León 1999). The baseline document from 1997 (the first year after the war ended) identified the administration of justice and citizen security as one of the main issues that needed to be tackled in order to build peace. The proposal advocated for increased access to justice in the rural areas and a transformation of public security institutions such as the police, the office of the attorney general and the judiciary. These proposals were complementary to the mainstream SSR approach in the peace agreement that envisioned – similar to the Salvadorean experience – a new civilian police, the reduction of the armed forces, and a new mandate with the sole responsibility of protecting the borders, alongside DDR of the small remaining guerrilla groups and strengthening the judiciary (de León and Sagone 2005). Supported by international donors, civil society organizations formed an advisory board for security policies (Consejo Asesor de Seguridad). The influence of the advisory board depended both on the willingness of the government to take this advice seriously and on pressure from international donors. Despite the significant power asymmetry, the cooperation between these local and international actors led to the establishment of the International Commission against Impunity in Guatemala (CICIG in its Spanish acronym) in 2008. During the following years, significant reforms were made to the public attorney's office and the judiciary. However, when these reforms led to formal accusations against the still-powerful economic, military, and political elites, CICIG's mandate was not prolonged, its personnel had to leave the country, and reform-oriented local actors went into exile (Gutiérrez 2016; Open Society Justice Initiative 2016). This example shows that participatory approaches are imported but need to be implemented and not subdued to existing power relations.

Second, SSR is a complex and long-term process that must be comprehensive, including the judiciary as a main link between the state and society. The experience of El Salvador – a rather successful peace process in terms of war termination – provides evidence about how an incomplete reform process and a lack of accountability for past human rights violations does not reduce violence but shifts it from the political arena to society. The process of demobilization went rather smoothly; other reforms in the Chapultepec Peace Accord of 1992 were designed to fundamentally change the integrated repressive system of the past via an evaluation of past behaviour and the dismissal of those individuals responsible for human rights violations (vetting), changes in mandate, and judicial independence. The reduction of the military's manpower and the reform of its mandate, as well as the establishment of the new civilian police force, took longer and were severely undermined by the right-wing government's 'moral panic' regarding public security and the inclusion of the military in public security operations (Kurtenbach and Reder 2021). Judicial reform was not a priority for the Nationalist Republican Alliance government and was made difficult by the second amnesty law, which rendered useless the recommendations of the Truth Commission, such as the vetting of high court justices. However, local and international human rights organizations advocated for change and against impunity for past atrocities, keeping the topic on the political agenda. Financial and technical support for judicial reforms came from the US Agency for International Development (USAID), with its strong focus on training, intended to increase the capacities of judges, along with professionalizing judges and other judicial personnel and modernizing the criminal and civil codes. Gradual change in the judiciary started in 2009 with the election of five independent judges, four of whom became members of the Constitutional Court. In 2016 these efforts seemed to bear fruit when the Constitutional Court declared the amnesty law of 1993 unconstitutional, bringing back some paradigmatic cases such as the massacre of El Mozote to the courts (Cerqueira and Arteaga 2016; Kurtenbach 2019).

Finally, post-war reforms do not happen in a political vacuum – there is no new beginning from scratch. Despite high hopes that the end of war will bring fundamental change and a better future, empirical evidence shows that a war's end is 'unlikely to see a clean break from violence to consent, from theft to production, from repression to democracy, or from impunity to accountability' (Keen 2000, 10). Even when fundamental reforms are envisioned in peace agreements, they will interact with existing structures and behaviours shaped by history, culture, and the experience of war and widespread violence (Wood 2008; Arjona 2014; Ansorg and Kurtenbach 2017). South Sudan is a case in point here. Even though the country's independence provided a clean break from previous institutional and power structures as part of Sudan, it continued to suffer from similar internal struggles and fractionalization, which eventually led to a renewed war. Hence, the end of war is not necessarily a critical juncture where profound change happens in a short period of time (Capoccia 2016) but can also favour path-dependent developments or fortify existing structures. Due to their direct and indirect participation in the war, institutions within the security and justice system (police, military, judiciary) are extremely important for reform processes and need to be analysed in their interaction and not separately.

Experiences on the ground show that international donors can support SSR at the intersection between state and society but should not be in the driver's seat. Top-down and state-centred approaches do not work either in the short term or in the long term. However, staying out of conflict-ridden and violent contexts is not an option from the perspective of international human rights norms, humanitarian law, and the responsibility to protect – and is often specifically requested by actors on the ground. However, international donors should be more resolute in their dedication to the normative frame of SSR – human rights, inclusion, accountability – as well as humbler, by supporting, monitoring, and accompanying local reform efforts. Knowledge exchange between international, national, and local-oriented actors can be a first step to assess the specific security and justice sector and identify institutions that work as well as those in need of reform. The viability and scope of reforms will depend on historic legacies as well as power relations between actors satisfied with the status quo and those who are reform-oriented.

6.3 Avenues for Future Research

Future research needs to include conceptual and more practical challenges. First, two aspects are of conceptual importance: greater contextualization, and what we consider 'decolonization of SSR'.

Contextualization goes beyond the prescription of norms and guidelines of the security sector. While norms are important, their inclusion needs to be based on a careful analysis and acknowledgement of local power relations and historical trajectories. On this basis, pathways to reform, obstacles, and opportunities need to be identified. Related to that is the regional environment of many post-war countries. As the examples of Sierra Leone and Iraq show, regional interactions influencing the reform process can be either conducive or non-conducive to the reform efforts (Almohamad, Kirchschlager, and Kurtenbach 2020). Therefore, context needs to be acknowledged at the local, national, regional, and international levels, and different patterns of transition (political pacts versus military victories) and the degree of international interventions fundamentally shape the outcome of SSR.

Finally, we need to acknowledge that knowledge and practice continue to be informed by epistemological assumptions that are deeply rooted in colonial history and colonial rule (Ansorg 2019). Policies in the Global North on development and international cooperation, particularly when it comes to post-war countries, still evince an idea of racial and civilizational hierarchy. These epistemological assumptions are inherently problematic and they transfer a sense of the world that ignores many aspects that are essential to the history, politics, and societies in the Global South. Thus, a further step in the evolution of post-war SSR can be an approach to decolonize reform aspects: to radically question the origins of knowledge and practice of SSR and to centre efforts more in the communities most affected by reform. This might include a decolonization of knowledge on SSR and a departure from the idea of 'making their security sector look more like our security sector' (Jackson 2018, 5). It could also include a change in practice, and a re-centring of reform towards the Global South, including the way that international donors fund programmes. This may require a fundamental reconsideration of foreign policy and a critical discussion of any intended and unintended effects of intervention. However, this does not imply that peacebuilding is not normatively embedded. External support for peace and for an inclusive and accountable security sector needs to emphasize violence reduction, individual, and collective human rights, as well as constructive conflict transformation. These are not Western values but core functions of every political and societal order. Otherwise, existing power relations and brute force will determine the fate in post-war societies.

On a more practical side, future research needs to compile data on relevant topics of SSR more systematically. More and better data is required on violence beyond armed conflict and the state. While there are some interesting projects under way at the Uppsala Data program and ACLED, these cover only parts of the Global South and started only recently – 1989 at the earliest. We also need better data on human rights, women, and ethnic participation in SSR beyond mere quantitative representation in the police, the military, or the judiciary. This data can help us to analyse specific challenges of SSR in a more fine-grained manner across time and space.

References

Abrahamsen R. (2016) Exporting Decentred Security Governance: The Tensions of Security Sector Reform. *Global Crime* **17**(3–4), 281–95. https://doi.org/10.1080/17440572.2016.1197507.

Abrahamsen R. and Williams M. C. (2009) Security beyond the State: Global Security Assemblages in International Politics. *International Political Sociology* **3**(1), 1–17. https://doi.org/10.1111/j.1749-5687.2008.00060.x.

Acemoglu D. and Robinson J. A. (2023) Weak, Despotic, or Inclusive? How State Type Emerges from State versus Civil Society Competition. *American Political Science Review*, **117**(2):407–20. https://doi.org/10.1017/S0003055422000740.

Albrecht P. and Jackson P. (2014) State-Building through Security Sector Reform: The UK Intervention in Sierra Leone. *Peacebuilding* **2**(1), 83–99. https://doi.org/10.1080/21647259.2013.866460.

Albrecht P. and Kyed H. M. (eds.) (2015) *Policing and the Politics of Order-Making*. Law, Development and Globalization. Abingdon: Routledge.

Albrecht P. and Wiuff Moe L. (2015) The Simultaneity of Authority in Hybrid Orders. *Peacebuilding* **3**(1), 1–16. https://doi.org/10.1080/21647259.2014.928551.

Almohamad S., Kirchschlager M. A. and Kurtenbach S. (2020) Peacebuilding after War and Violence – Neighbourhood Matters. *GIGA Working Paper*, no. 324. www.giga-hamburg.de/de/publikationen/22561100-peacebuilding-after-violence-neighbourhood-matters/.

Andersen L. R. (2011) Security Sector Reform and the Dilemmas of Liberal Peacebuilding. *DIIS Working Paper*, no. 31. Copenhagen: Danish Institute for International Studies (DIIS). www.jstor.com/stable/resrep13456.

Andreas P. and Greenhill K. M. (2010) Introduction: The Politics of Numbers. In *Sex, Drugs, and Body Counts: The Politics of Numbers in Global Crime and Conflict*. Ithaca: Cornell University Press, 1–22.

Ansorg N. (2019) Decolonising Security Sector Reform in Fragile Countries in the Global South. Keynote address at the Workshop 'Security Sector Reform in Fragile Contexts – What Works Best, Where and When?' Federal Academy for Security Policy and GIZ, Berlin.

Ansorg N. and Gordon E. (2019) Co-Operation, Contestation and Complexity in Post-Conflict Security Sector Reform. *Journal of Intervention and Statebuilding* **13**(1), 2–24. https://doi.org/10.1080/17502977.2018.1516392.

Ansorg N. and Haastrup T. (2018) Gender and the EU's Support for Security Sector Reform in Fragile Contexts: Gender & the EU's Support to SSR. *Journal of Common Market Studies*, **56**(5): 1127–43. https://doi.org/10.1111/jcms.12716.

Ansorg N. and Kurtenbach S. (2017) Introduction: Institutional Reforms and Peace Building. In Ansorg N. and Kurtenbach S. (eds.), *Institutional Reforms and Peacebuilding: Change, Path-Dependency and Societal Divisions in Post-War Communities*. Abingdon: Routledge, 1–18.

2022. Reforma al sector seguridad después de la guerra: lo que se sabe y lo que se desconoce de los casos al rededor del mundo. 5. Documento de Trabajo. Bogotá: CAPAZ. www.instituto-capaz.org/wp-content/uploads/2022/04/DT-5-2022_Nadine-y-Sabine-web-ok.pdf.

Argueta O. (2012). Private Security in Guatemala: Pathway to Its Proliferation. *Bulletin of Latin American Research* **31**(3), 320–35.

Arjona A. (2014) Wartime Institutions: A Research Agenda. *Journal of Conflict Resolution* **58**(8), 1360–89. https://doi.org/10.1177/0022002714547904.

Arjona A., Kasfir N. and Mampilly Z. (eds.) (2015) *Rebel Governance in Civil War*. New York: Cambridge University Press.

Bagayoko N., Hutchful E. and Luckham, R. (2016) Hybrid Security Governance in Africa: Rethinking the Foundations of Security, Justice and Legitimate Public Authority. *Conflict, Security & Development* **16** (1), 1–32. https://doi.org/10.1080/14678802.2016.1136137.

Baker B. (2010) The Future Is Non-State. In Sedra M. (ed.), *The Future of Security Sector Reform*. Waterloo: The Centre for International Governance Innovation, 208–28.

Baker B. and Scheye E. (2007) Multi-Layered Justice and Security Delivery in Post-Conflict and Fragile States: Analysis. *Conflict, Security & Development* **7**(4), 503–28. https://doi.org/10.1080/14678800701692944.

Bara C., Deglow A. and van Baalen S. (2021) Civil War Recurrence and Postwar Violence: Toward an Integrated Research Agenda. *European Journal of International Relations* **27**(3), 913–35. https://doi.org/10.1177/13540661211006443.

Barnes N. (2017) Criminal Politics: An Integrated Approach to the Study of Organized Crime, Politics, and Violence. *Perspectives on Politics* **15**(04), 967–87. https://doi.org/10.1017/S1537592717002110.

Berg L.-A. (2020) Civil–Military Relations and Civil War Recurrence: Security Forces in Postwar Politics. *Journal of Conflict Resolution* **64**(7–8), 1307–34. https://doi.org/10.1177/0022002720903356.

Berg, L.-A. (2022) *Governing Security After War. The Politics of Institutional Change in the Security Sector*. New York: Oxford University Press.

Berquist C., Peñaranda R. and Sánchez G. (eds.) (2001) *Violence in Colombia 1990–2000: Waging War and Negotiating Peace*. Wilmington: Scholarly Resources Books.

Binningsbø H.-M., Buhaug H. and Dahl M. (2012) Determinants of Civil War Recurrence. Paper for the 20th Annual Norwegian Political Science Conference, Trondheim.

Birke Daniels K. and Kurtenbach S. (eds.) (2021) *Entanglements of Peace: Reflections on the Long Road of Transformation in Colombia*. Bogotá: FESCOL.

Bolte B., Joo M. M. and Mukherjee B. (2021) Security Consolidation in the Aftermath of Civil War: Explaining the Fates of Victorious Militias. *Journal of Conflict Resolution*. https://doi.org/10.1177/0022002721995528.

Boulding E. (2000) *Cultures of Peace: The Hidden Side of History*. Syracuse: Syracuse University Press.

Bouvier V. M. (2009) *Colombia: Building Peace in a Time of War*. 1st ed. Washington, DC: US Institute of Peace Press.

Brigg M. (2016) Relational Peacebuilding: Promise beyond Crisis. In Debiel T., Held T. and Schneckener U. (eds.), *Peacebuilding in Crisis: Rethinking Paradigms and Practices of Transnational Cooperation*. New York: Routledge, 56–9.

Brown M. A. (2020) The Spatial Turn, Reification and Relational Epistemologies in ‘Knowing about’ Security and Peace. *Cooperation and Conflict* **55**(4), 421–41.

Bruneau T. C. and Matei C. F. (2008) Towards a New Conceptualization of Democratization and Civil-Military Relations. *Democratization* **15**(5), 909–29. https://doi.org/10.1080/13510340802362505.

Call C. T. (2012) *Why Peace Fails: The Causes and Prevention of Civil War Recurrence*. Washington, DC: Georgetown University Press.

Call C. T. and Stanley W. (2001) Protecting the People: Public Security Choices after Civil Wars. *Global Governance* **7**, 151–72.

Cao L. and Zhao J. S. (2005) Confidence in the Police in Latin America. *Journal of Criminal Justice* **33**(5), 403–12. https://doi.org/10.1016/j.jcrimjus.2005.06.009.

Caparini M. (2006) Applying a Security Governance Perspective to the Privatisation of Security. In Bryden A. and Caparini M. (eds.), *Private Actors and Security Governance*, Muenster: Lit & DCAF, 263–82.

Capoccia G. (2016) When Do Institutions ‘Bite’? Historical Institutionalism and the Politics of Institutional Change. *Comparative Political Studies* **49**(8), 1095–127. https://doi.org/10.1177/0010414015626449.

Carey S. C. and González B. (2020) The Legacy of War: The Effect of Militias on Postwar Repression. *Conflict Management and Peace Science*. https://doi.org/10.1177/0738894219899006.

Cerqueira D. and Arteaga L. (2016) Challenging the Amnesty Law in El Salvador: Domestic and International Alternatives to Bring an End to Impunity. *Legal Analysis*. Due Process of Law Foundation. www.dplf.org/sites/default/files/amnesty_law-final-24june.pdf.

Chaves P., Aarts N. and van Bommel S. (2020) Self-Organization for Everyday Peacebuilding: The Guardia Indígena from Northern Cauca, Colombia. *Security Dialogue* **51**(1), 39–59. https://doi.org/10.1177/0967010619889471.

Clausen M.-L. and Albrecht P. (2021) Interventions since the Cold War: From Statebuilding to Stabilization. *International Affairs* **97**(4), 1203–20. https://doi.org/10.1093/ia/iiab084.

Collantes-Celador G. (2006) Police Reform: Peacebuilding through 'Democratic Policing'? In Chandler D. (ed.), *Peace without Politics? Ten Years of State-Building in Bosnia*. Abingdon: Routledge, 58–70.

Comisión para el Esclarecimiento de la Verdad, la Convivencia y la No Repetición (2022) Hay Futuro Si Hay Verdad. Hasta La Guerra Tiene Límites. Violaciones de Los Derechos Humanos, Infracciones al Derecho Internacional Humanitario y Responsabilidades Colectivas. Informe Final. Bogotá. www.comisiondelaverdad.co/hay-futuro-si-hay-verdad.

Coning C. de (2018) Adaptive Peacebuilding. *International Affairs* **94**(2), 301–17. https://doi.org/10.1093/ia/iix251.

Croissant A. (2006) International Interim Governments, Democratization, and Post-Conflict Peace-Building: Lessons from Cambodia and East Timor. *Strategic Insights* **5**(1). http://calhoun.nps.edu/bitstream/handle/10945/11073/CroissantJan06.pdf?sequence=1.

Croissant A. and Kuehn D. (eds.) (2017) *Reforming Civil-Military Relations in New Democracies*. Cham: Springer International. https://doi.org/10.1007/978-3-319-53189-2.

Croissant A., Kühn D., Chambers P. W., Völkel P. and Wolf S. O. (2011) Theorizing Civilian Control of the Military in Emerging Democracies: Agency, Structure and Institutional Change. *Zeitschrift Für Vergleichende Politikwissenschaft* **5**(1), 75–98. https://doi.org/10.1007/s12286-011-0101-6.

Cruz J. M. (2015) Police Misconduct and Political Legitimacy in Central America. *Journal of Latin American Studies* **47**(02), 251–83. https://doi.org/10.1017/S0022216X15000085.

Daly S. Z. (2014) The Dark Side of Power-Sharing: Middle Managers and Civil War Recurrence. *Comparative Politics* **46**(3), 333–53.

Dancy G. (2018) Deals with the Devil? Conflict Amnesties, Civil War, and Sustainable Peace. *International Organization* **72**(2), 387–421. https://doi.org/10.1017/S0020818318000012.

Dancy G. and Wiebelhaus-Brahm E. (2018) The Impact of Criminal Prosecutions during Intrastate Conflict. *Journal of Peace Research* **55**(1), 47–61. https://doi.org/10.1177/0022343317732614.

Daniels L.-A. (2020) How and When Amnesty during Conflict Affects Conflict Termination. *Journal of Conflict Resolution* **64**(9), 1612–37. https://doi.org/10.1177/0022002720909884.

Darby J. (2006) Post-Accord Violence in a Changing World. In *Violence and Reconstruction*. Notre Dame: University of Notre Dame Press, 143–60.

Day A., von Billerbeck S., Tansey O. and Al Maleh A. (2021) Peacebuilding and Authoritarianism: The Unintended Consequences of UN Engagement in Post-Conflict Settings. New York: United Nations University Centre for Policy Research. http://collections.unu.edu/eserv/UNU:8035/UNU_Peacebuilding_FINAL_WEB.pdf.

DCAF (2006) United Nations Approaches to Security Sector Reform. www.dcaf.ch/sites/default/files/publications/documents/ev_bratislava_060707_UN_paper.pdf.

(2019) *Civil Society*. SSR Backgrounder Series. Geneva: DCAF.

Dearing M. P. (2022) *Militia Order in Afghanistan: Guardians or Gangsters?* 1st ed. London: Routledge. https://doi.org/10.4324/9781003149071.

Derksen D. (2015) The Politics of Disarmament and Rearmament in Afghanistan. Peace Works 110. Washington, DC: USIP. www.usip.org/publications/2015/05/politics-disarmament-and-rearmament-afghanistan.

Diehl P. F. (2016) Exploring Peace: Looking beyond War and Negative Peace. *International Studies Quarterly* **60**(1), 1–10. https://doi.org/10.1093/isq/sqw005.

Donais T. (2018) Security Sector Reform and the Challenge of Vertical Integration. *Journal of Intervention and Statebuilding* **12**(1), 31–47. https://doi.org/10.1080/17502977.2018.1426681.

Donais T. and Barbak A. (2021) The Rule of Law, the Local Turn, and Re-Thinking Accountability in Security Sector Reform Processes. *Peacebuilding*, 1–16. https://doi.org/10.1080/21647259.2021.1895622.

Doyle M. W. and Sambanis N. (2000) International Peacebuilding: A Theoretical and Quantitative Analysis. *The American Political Science Review* **94**(4), 779–801.

Duran-Martinez A. (2015) To Kill and Tell? State Power, Criminal Competition, and Drug Violence. *Journal of Conflict Resolution* **59**(8), 1377–402. https://doi.org/10.1177/0022002715587047.

Elias N. (1987) The Retreat of Sociologists into the Present. *Theory, Culture & Society* **4**, 223–47.

European Commission for the Efficiency of Justice (CEPEJ) (2018) European Judicial Systems Efficiency and Quality of Justice. CEPEJ Studies No. 26. Strasbourg. https://rm.coe.int/rapport-avec-couv-18-09-2018-en/16808def9c.

European Court of Auditors (2015) The EU Police Mission in Afghanistan: Mixed Results. Special Report. Luxembourg: European Court of Auditors. www.eca.europa.eu/Lists/ECADocuments/SR15_07/SR_EUPOL_AFGHANISTAN_EN.pdf.

Felbab-Brown V. (2016) Hurray for Militias? Not So Fast: Lessons from the Afghan Local Police Experience. *Small Wars & Insurgencies* **27**(2), 258–81. https://doi.org/DOI:10.1080/09592318.2015.1129169.

Firchow P. (2018) *Reclaiming Everyday Peace: Local Voices in Measurement and Evaluation after War*. Cambridge: Cambridge University Press. https://doi.org/10.1017/9781108236140.

Flores T. E. and Nooruddin I. (2012) The Effect of Elections on Postconflict Peace and Reconstruction. *The Journal of Politics* **74**(02), 558–70. https://doi.org/10.1017/S0022381611001733.

Freeman M. (2009) *Necessary Evils: Amnesties and the Search for Justice*. Cambridge: Cambridge University Press. https://doi.org/10.1017/CBO9780511691850.

Galtung J. (1981) Social Cosmology and the Concept of Peace. *Journal of Peace Research* **18**(2), 183–99.

GAO (US Government Accountability Office) (2008) Plan Colombia. Report to the Honorable Joseph R. Biden, Jr., Chairman, Committee on Foreign Relations, U.S. Senate. www.gao.gov/assets/290/282511.pdf.

Gartner R. and Kennedy L. (2018) War and Postwar Violence. *Crime and Justice* **47**(1), 1–67. https://doi.org/10.1086/696649.

George A. L. and Bennett A. (2005) *Case Studies and Theory Development in the Social Sciences*. Cambridge, MA: MIT Press.

Giustozzi A. (2008) The Art of Coercion: Armed Force in the Context of State Building. *Crisis States Research Centre (CSRC) Seminar*. **10**. www.lse.ac.uk/internationalDevelopment/research/crisisStates/download/seminars/GiustozziDec10Revised.pdf.

(2012a) Afghanistan: 'Chaotic' Peacekeeping and DDRGi. In Giustozzi A. (ed.), *Post-Conflict Disarmament, Demobilization and Reintegration: Bringing State-Building Back In*. Burlington: Ashgate, 57–71.

(ed.) (2012b) *Post-Conflict Disarmament, Demobilization and Reintegration. Bringing the State-Building Back In*. Global Security in a Changing World. Farnham: Ashgate.

(2019) *The Taliban at War 2001–2018*. London: C Hurst.

Gleditsch N. P., Wallensteen P., Eriksson M., Sollenberg M. and Strand H. (2002a) Armed Conflict 1946–2001: A New Dataset. *Journal of Peace Research* **39**(5), 615–37.

(2002b) Armed Conflict 1946–2001: A New Dataset. *Journal of Peace Research* **39**(5), 615–37. https://doi.org/10.1177/0022343302039005007.

Global Witness (2019) Enemies of the State. www.globalwitness.org/en/campaigns/environmental-activists/enemies-state/.

Goertz G. (2020) Peace: The Elusive Dependent Variable and Policy Goal. *Perspectives on Politics* **18**(1), 200–4. https://doi.org/10.1017/S1537592719004511.

Goldsmith A. (2005) Police Reform and the Problem of Trust. *Theoretical Criminology* **9**(4), 443–70. https://doi.org/10.1177/1362480605057727.

González González F. E. (2014) *Poder y Violencia En Colombia*. Colección Territorio, Poder y Conflicto. Bogotá: CINEP.

Goodhand J. (2009) *Bandits, Borderlands and Opium Wars: Afghan State-Building Viewed from the Margins. DIIS Working Paper*, no. 2009/26. Copenhagen: Danish Institute for International Studies.

Gordon E., McHugh C. and Townsley J. (2021) Risks versus Transformational Opportunities in Gender-Responsive Security Sector Reform. *Journal of Global Security Studies* **6**(2), ogaa028. https://doi.org/10.1093/jogss/ogaa028.

Gossman P. and Kline P. (2015) *'Today We Shall All Die': Afghanistan's Strongmen and the Legacy of Impunity*. Edited by Human Rights Watch. Human Rights Watch (Organization). New York: Human Rights Watch.

Grabendorff W. (2009) *Limited Security Sector Reform in Colombia*. Security Sector Reform in Challenging Environments. Geneva: Geneva Centre for the Democratic Control of Armed Forces. www.dcaf.ch/content/download/36932/529081/version/1/file/Ch03_Colombia_12Oct.pdf.

Gray J. L. and Strasheim J. (2016) Security Sector Reform, Ethnic Representation and Perceptions of Safety: Evidence from Kosovo. *Civil Wars* **18**(3), 338–58. https://doi.org/10.1080/13698249.2016.1215636.

Groot T. de and Regilme S. S. F. (2022) Private Military and Security Companies and the Militarization of Humanitarianism. *Journal of*

Developing Societies **38**(1), 50–80. https://doi.org/10.1177/0169796X211066874.

Grupo de Trabajo FIP – FESCOL (2021) Liderazgo Civil y Transformación de La Policía. Recomendaciones Para La Governanza de Seguridad. www.ideaspaz.org/publications/posts/2039.

Gutiérrez E. (2016) Guatemala Fuera de Control. La CICIG y La Lucha Contra La Impunidad. *Nueva Sociedad* **263** (Mayo–Junio), 81–95.

Gutiérrez Sanín F. and González Peña A. (2012) Colombia's Paramilitary DDR and Its Limits. In Giustozzi A. (ed.), *Post-Conflict Disarmament, Demobilizaton and Reintegration. Bringing State-Building Back In*. Burlington: Ashgate, 113–32.

Hartzell C. A. and Hoddie M. (2007) *Crafting Peace: Power-Sharing Institutions and the Negotiated Settlement of Civil Wars*. University Park, PA: Pennsylvania State University Press.

(2011) Missed Opportunities. The Impact of DDR on SSR in Afghanistan. 270. Special Report. Washington, DC: USIP. www.usip.org/sites/default/files/resources/SR270-Missed_Opportunities.pdf.

Hartzell C., Hoddie M. and Rothchild D. (2001) Stabilizing the Peace after Civil War: An Investigation of Some Key Variables. *International Organization* **55**(01), 183–208. https://doi.org/10.1162/002081801551450.

Hartzell, C. and Hoddie M. (2003) Institutionalizing Peace: Power Sharing and Post-Civil War Conflict Management. *American Journal of Political Science* **47**(2): 318–32.

Högbladh, S. (2011) Peace Agreements 1975-2011 - Updating the UCDP Peace Agreement Dataset. In Pettersson T. and Themnér L. (eds.), *States in Armed Conflict 2011*. Uppsala: Uppsala University, Dept. of Peace and Conflict Research, 39–56.

Hohe T. (2003) Justice without Judiciary in East Timor. *Conflict, Security & Development* **3**(3), 335–57. https://doi.org/10.1080/1467880032000151626.

Holdt K. von (2012) The Violence of Order, Orders of Violence: Between Fanon and Bourdieu. *Current Sociology* **61**(2), 112–31. https://doi.org/10.1177/0011392112456492.

Holohan A. (2016) Peacebuilding and SSR in Kosovo: An Interactionist Perspective. *Global Crime* **17**(3–4), 331–51. https://doi.org/10.1080/17440572.2016.1197508.

Human Rights Watch (ed.) (2005) *Blood-Stained Hands: Past Atrocities in Kabul and Afghanistan's Legacy of Impunity*. New York: Human Rights Watch.

Huneeus A. (2013) International Criminal Law by Other Means: The Quasi-Criminal Jurisdiction of the Human Rights Courts. *The American Journal of International Law* **107**(1), 1–44.

INDEPAZ (2020) Registro de Líderes y Personas Defensoras de DDHH Asesinadas Desde La Firma de Los Acuerdos de Paz Del 24/11/2016 al 15/07/2020. Informe Especial. Bogotá: Instituo de estudios para el desarrollo y la paz. www.indepaz.org.co/wp-content/uploads/2020/07/Informe-Especial-Asesinato-lideres-sociales-Nov2016-Jul2020-Indepaz.pdf.

Jabri V. (2013) Peacebuilding, the Local and the International: A Colonial or a Postcolonial Rationality? *Peacebuilding* **1**(1), 3–16. https://doi.org/10.1080/21647259.2013.756253.

Jackson P. (2018) Introduction: Second-Generation Security Sector Reform. *Journal of Intervention and Statebuilding* **12**(1), 1–10. https://doi.org/10.1080/17502977.2018.1426384.

Joshi M., Quinn J. M. and Regan P. M. (2015) Annualized Implementation Data on Comprehensive Intrastate Peace Accords, 1989–2012. *Journal of Peace Research* **52**(4), 551–62. https://doi.org/10.1177/0022343314567486.

Julian R., Bliesemann de Guevara B. and Redhead R. (2019) From Expert to Experiential Knowledge: Exploring the Inclusion of Local Experiences in Understanding Violence in Conflict. *Peacebuilding* **7**(2), 210–25. https://doi.org/10.1080/21647259.2019.1594572.

Kalyvas S. N. (2006) *The Logic of Violence in Civil War*. 1st ed. Cambridge: Cambridge University Press.

Kaplan O. and Nussio E. (2018) Community Counts: The Social Reintegration of Ex-Combatants in Colombia. *Conflict Management and Peace Science* **35**(2), 132–53. https://doi.org/10.1177/0738894215614506.

Keen D. (2000) War and Peace: What's the Difference? *International Peacekeeping* **7**(4), 1–22. https://doi.org/10.1080/13533310008413860.

Kim H. and Sikkink K. (2010) Explaining the Deterrence Effect of Human Rights Prosecutions for Transitional Countries: Explaining the Deterrence Effects of Human Rights. *International Studies Quarterly* **54**(4), 939–63. https://doi.org/10.1111/j.1468-2478.2010.00621.x.

Köllner P., Sil R. and Ahram A. I. (2018) *Comparative Area Studies*. Vol. 1. Oxford: Oxford University Press. https://doi.org/10.1093/oso/9780190846374.003.0001.

Kreutz J. (2010) How and When Armed Conflicts End: Introducing the UCDP Conflict Termination Dataset. *Journal of Peace Research* **47**(2), 243–50.

Kurtenbach S. (2013) The 'Happy Outcomes' May Not Come at All – Postwar Violence in Central America. *Civil Wars* **15**(sup1), 105–22. https://doi.org/10.1080/13698249.2013.850884.

(2017a) No One Size Fits All – A Global Approach to Peace. *GIGA Focus Global*, no. 4. www.giga-hamburg.de/en/publications/giga-focus/no-one-size-fits-all-a-global-approach-to-peace.

(2017b) The Challenges of Institutional Reforms in the Midst of War: Lessons from Colombia. In Ansorg N. and Kurtenbach S. (eds.) *Institutional Reforms and Peacebuilding Change, Path-Dependency and Societal Divisions in Post-War Communities*. Conflict, Development and Peacebuilding. London: Routledge, 83–102.

(2019) Judicial Reform – A Neglected Dimension of SSR in El Salvador. *Journal of Intervention and Statebuilding* **13**(1), 57–74. https://doi.org/10.1080/17502977.2018.1517112.

(2020) Envisioning Peace|Transforming Conflict: A Global Approach to Peace. In Carey H. F. (ed.), *Peacebuilding Paradigms. The Impact of Theoretical Diversity on Implementing Sustainable Peace*. Cambridge: Cambridge University Press, 241–54.

Kurtenbach S. and Reder D. (2021) El Salvador: Old Habits Die Hard. In Kuehn D. and Levy Y. (eds.), *Mobilizing Force: Linking Security Threats, Militarization, and Civilian Control*. Boulder: Lynne Rienner, 117–38.

Kyed H. M. and Albrecht P. (2015) Introduction. Policing and the Politics of Order Making on the Urban Margins. In Kyed H. M. and Albrecht P. (eds.), *Policing and the Politics of Order-Making*. Abingdon: Routledge Taylor & Francis Group, 1–23.

Lake D. A. and Rothchild D. (1996) Containing Fear: The Origins and Management of Ethnic Conflict. *International Security* **21**(2), 41–75. https://doi.org/10.1162/isec.21.2.41.

Leander A. (2003) Wars and the Un-Making of States Taking Tilly Seriously in the Contemporary World. In Guzzini S. and Jung D. (eds.), *Contemporary Security Analysis and Copenhagen Peace Research*. London: Routledge, 69–80.

(2005) The Market for Force and Public Security: The Destabilizing Consequences of Private Military Companies. *Journal of Peace Research* **42**(5), 605–22. https://doi.org/10.1177/0022343305056237.

León C. R. de and Sagone I. (2005) *Guatemala*. San José: Fundación Arias.

Lessing B. (2021) Conceptualizing Criminal Governance. *Perspectives on Politics* **19**(3), 854–73. https://doi.org/10.1017/S1537592720001243.

Lewis D., Heathershaw J. and Megoran N. (2018) Illiberal Peace? Authoritarian Modes of Conflict Management. *Cooperation and Conflict* **53**(4), 486–506.

Luckham R. (2015) Whose Security? Building Inclusive and Secure Societies in an Unequal and Insecure World. Evidence Report. Addressing and Mitigating Violence. Koninklijke Brill NV. https://doi.org/10.1163/2210-7975_HRD-0148-2015068.

(2017) Whose Violence, Whose Security? Can Violence Reduction and Security Work for Poor, Excluded and Vulnerable People? *Peacebuilding* **5**(2), 99–117. https://doi.org/10.1080/21647259.2016.1277009.

MacGinty R. (2021) *Everyday Peace: How So-Called Ordinary People Can Disrupt Violent Conflict*. Studies in Strategic Peacebuilding. Oxford: Oxford University Press.

Mattes, M. and Savun B. (2009) Fostering Peace after Civil War: Commitment Problems and Agreement Design. *International Studies Quarterly* **53**(3), 737–59. https://doi.org/10.1111/j.1468-2478.2009.00554.x.

McCandless E. (2020) Resilient Social Contracts and Peace: Towards a Needed Reconceptualization. *Journal of Intervention and Statebuilding* **14**(1), 1–21. https://doi.org/10.1080/17502977.2019.1682925.

McCandless E., Abitbol E. and Donais T. (2015) Vertical Integration: A Dynamic Practice Promoting Transformative Peacebuilding. *Journal of Peacebuilding & Development* **10**(1), 1–9. https://doi.org/10.1080/15423166.2015.1014268.

McFate S. (2016) PMSCs in International Security Sector Reform. In Abrahamsen R. and Leander A. (eds.), *Routledge Handbook of Private Security Studies*. Abingdon: Routledge, 118–27.

Meagher K. (2012) The Strength of Weak States? Non-State Security Forces and Hybrid Governance in Africa. *Development and Change* **43**(5): 1073–101. http://onlinelibrary.wiley.com/doi/10.1111/j.1467-7660.2012.01794.x/full.

Melo Moreno V. and Centro de Memoria Histórica (Colombia) (2018) *Todo pasó frente a nuestros ojos: el genocidio de la Unión Patriótica, 1984–2002*.

Migdal J. S. (2001) *State in Society: Studying How States and Societies Transform and Constitute One Another*. Cambridge: Cambridge University Press.

Millar G. (2020) Preserving the Everyday: Pre-Political Agency in Peacebuilding Theory. *Cooperation and Conflict*. https://doi.org/10.1177/0010836720904390.

(2021) Ambition and Ambivalence: Reconsidering Positive Peace as a Trans-Scalar Peace System. *Journal of Peace Research* **58**(4), 640–54. https://doi.org/10.1177/0022343320941909.

Moodie E. (2010) *El Salvador in the Aftermath of Peace: Crime, Uncertainty, and the Transition to Democracy*. Philadelphia: Pennsylvania State University Press.

Munive J. and Stepputat F. (2015) Rethinking Disarmament, Demobilization and Reintegration Programs. *Stability: International Journal of Security & Development* **4**(1), 1–13. https://doi.org/10.5334/sta.go.

Muthien B. (2018) Human Security and Intersectional Oppressions. Women in South Africa. In Reardon B. and Hans A. (eds.), *The Gender Imperative: Human Security vs State Security*, 2nd ed. New Delhi: Routledge India. https://doi.org/10.4324/9780429452130.

Nadery A. N. (2007) Peace or Justice? Transitional Justice in Afghanistan. *International Journal of Transitional Justice* **1**(1), 173–9. https://doi.org/10.1093/ijtj/ijm005.

Neild R. (2001) Democratic Police Reforms in War-Torn Societies. *Conflict, Security & Development* **1**(01), 21–43. https://doi.org/10.1080/14678800100590596.

Nielson, D. L. and Soberg Shugart M. (1999) Constitutional Change in Colombia. Policy Adjustment through Institutional Reform. *Comparative Political Studies* **32**(3), 313–41.

Nilsson M. and Jonsson C. (2022) Building Relational Peace: Police-Community Relations in Post-Accord Colombia. *Policing and Society*, 1–19. https://doi.org/10.1080/10439463.2022.2147175.

OECD (2005) Security System Reform and Governance. DAC Guidelines and Reference Series. Paris: OECD.

(2007) *The OECD DAC Handbook on Security System Reform: Supporting Security and Justice*. de l'OCDE.

Olivius E. and Åkebo M. (2021) Exploring Varieties of Peace: Advancing the Agenda. *Journal of Peacebuilding & Development* **16**(1), 3–8. https://doi.org/10.1177/1542316621995641.

Onoma A. K. (2014) Transition Regimes and Security Sector Reforms in Sierra Leone and Liberia. *The ANNALS of the American Academy of Political and Social Science* **656**(1), 136–53. https://doi.org/10.1177/0002716214545445.

Oosterveld W. and Galand R. (2012) Justice Reform, Security Sector Reform and Local Ownership. *Hague Journal on the Rule of Law* **4**(01), 194–209. https://doi.org/10.1017/S1876404512000115.

Open Society Justice Initiative (2016) Against the Odds. CICIG in Guatemala. New York. www.opensocietyfoundations.org/sites/default/files/against-odds-cicig-guatemala-20160321.pdf.

Ottmann, M. and Vüllers, J. (2015) The Power-Sharing Event Dataset (PSED): A New Dataset on the Promises and Practices of Power-Sharing in Post-Conflict Countries. *Conflict Management and Peace Science* **32**(3): 327–50.

Paffenholz T. (2021) Perpetual Peacebuilding: A New Paradigm to Move beyond the Linearity of Liberal Peacebuilding. *Journal of Intervention and Statebuilding* **15**(3), 367–85. https://doi.org/10.1080/17502977.2021.1925423.

Parlevliet M. (2017) Human Rights and Peacebuilding: Complementary and Contradictory, Complex and Contingent. *Journal of Human Rights Practice* **9**(3), 333–57. https://doi.org/10.1093/jhuman/hux032.

Pearce, J. (2016) The 'Violence Turn' in Peace Studies and Practice. *'Undeclared Wars' –Exploring a Peacebuilding Approach to Armed Social Violence. Berghof Handbook Dialogue Series*, 12, 31–40.

Pettersson T., Högbladh S. and Öberg M. (2019) Organized Violence, 1989–2018 and Peace Agreements. *Journal of Peace Research* **56**(4), 589–603. https://doi.org/10.1177/0022343319856046.

Piccolino G. (2015) Winning Wars, Building (Illiberal) Peace? The Rise (and Possible Fall) of a Victor's Peace in Rwanda and Sri Lanka. *Third World Quarterly* **36**(9), 1770–85. https://doi.org/10.1080/01436597.2015.1058150.

Policía Nacional de Colombia, Bogotá DC, Colombia, Ángel Uriel Hernández-González, Luce Marina Echeverri-Petti, Policía Nacional de Colombia, Bogotá DC, Colombia,Gonzalo Andrés Cortés-Olarte, and Policía Nacional de Colombia, Bogotá DC, Colombia. 2021. Caracterización, inclusión y participación de la mujer policía en Colombia. Análisis 1994–2021. *Revista Logos, Ciencia & Tecnología* **13**(3). https://doi.org/10.22335/rlct.v13i3.1445.

Prorok A. K. (2017) The (In)Compatibility of Peace and Justice? The International Criminal Court and Civil Conflict Termination. *International Organization* **71**(02), 213–43. https://doi.org/10.1017/S0020818317000078.

Reardon B. A. and Snauwaert D. T. (2014) *Betty A. Reardon: A Pioneer in Education for Peace and Human Rights*. Dordrecht: Springer.

Regan P. M. (2014) Bringing Peace Back In: Presidential Address to the Peace Science Society, 2013. *Conflict Management and Peace Science* **31**(4), 345–56. https://doi.org/10.1177/0738894214530852.

Reid R. and Muhammedally S. (2011) *'Just Don't Call It a Militia': Impunity, Militias, and the 'Afghan Local Police'*. New York: Human Rights Watch.

Richani N. (2002) *Systems of Violence: The Political Economy of War and Peace in Colombia*. Albany: State University of New York Press.

Romero M. (2003) *Paramilitares y autodefensas 1982–2003*. Bogotá: Planeta.

(2021) Reintegration of FARC-EP and Territorial Spaces: Possibilities, Obstacles, and Frustrations. In Birke Daniels K. and Kurtenbach S. (eds.), *Entanglement of Peace: Reflections on the Long Road of Transformation in Colombia*. Bogotá: FESCOL, 103–26.

Rubin B. R. (2003) Transitional Justice and Human Rights in Afghanistan. *International Affairs* **79**(3), 567–81. https://doi.org/10.1111/1468-2346.00323.

Sabaratnam M. (2013) Avatars of Eurocentrism in the Critique of the Liberal Peace. *Security Dialogue* **44**(3), 259–78. https://doi.org/10.1177/0967010613485870.

Scheye E. and McLean A. (2006) Enhancing the Delivery of Justice and Security in Fragile States. Paris: OECD.

Schroeder U. C. and Chappuis F. (2014) New Perspectives on Security Sector Reform: The Role of Local Agency and Domestic Politics. *International Peacekeeping* **21**(2), 133–48. https://doi.org/10.1080/13533312.2014.910401.

Schroeder U. C., Chappuis F. and Kocak D. (2014) Security Sector Reform and the Emergence of Hybrid Security Governance. *International Peacekeeping* **21**(2), 214–30. https://doi.org/10.1080/13533312.2014.910405.

Schubiger L. I. (2021) State Violence and Wartime Civilian Agency: Evidence from Peru. *The Journal of Politics* **83**(4), 1383–98. https://doi.org/10.1086/711720.

Sedra M. (2017) *Security Sector Reform in Conflict-Affected Countries: The Evolution of a Model*. Abingdon: Routledge Taylor & Francis Group.

(2018) Adapting Security Sector Reform to Ground-Level Realities: The Transition to a Second-Generation Model. *Journal of Intervention and Statebuilding* **12**(1), 48–63. https://doi.org/10.1080/17502977.2018.1426383.

Sen A. (2001) *Development as Freedom*. Oxford: Oxford University Press.

Sikkink K. (2014) Latin American Countries as Norm Protagonists of the Idea of International Human Rights. *Global Governance* **20**(3), 389–404.

Singh D. (2014) Corruption and Clientelism in the Lower Levels of the Afghan Police. *Conflict, Security and Development* **5**, 1467–8802. https://doi.org/10.1080/14678802.2014.963391.

Sjoberg L. (2014) *Gender, War, and Conflict*. Cambridge: Polity Press.

Steenkamp C. (2011) In the Shadows of War and Peace: Making Sense of Violence after Peace Accords. *Conflict, Security & Development* **11**(3), 357–83. https://doi.org/10.1080/14678802.2011.593813.

Stepputat F. (2018) Pragmatic Peace in Emerging Governscapes. *International Affairs* **94**(2), 399–416. https://doi.org/10.1093/ia/iix233.

Subedi D. B. (2014) Conflict, Combatants, and Cash: Economic Reintegration and Livelihoods of Ex-Combatants in Nepal. *World Development* **59**(July), 238–50. https://doi.org/10.1016/j.worlddev.2014.01.025.

Svensson I. (2009) Who Brings Which Peace? Neutral versus Biased Mediation and Institutional Peace Arrangements in Civil Wars. *Journal of Conflict Resolution* **53**(3), 446–69. https://doi.org/10.1177/0022002709332207.

Tapscott R. (2021) Vigilantes and the State: Understanding Violence through a Security Assemblages Approach. *Perspectives on Politics*, June, 1–16. https://doi.org/10.1017/S1537592721001134.

Tellez J. F. (2021) Land, Opportunism, and Displacement in Civil Wars: Evidence from Colombia. *American Political Science Review*, 1–16. https://doi.org/10.1017/S0003055421001003.

Terpstra N. (2020) Rebel Governance, Rebel Legitimacy, and External Intervention: Assessing Three Phases of Taliban Rule in Afghanistan. *Small Wars & Insurgencies* **31**(6), 1143–73. https://doi.org/10.1080/09592318.2020.1757916.

Themnér L. and Wallensteen P. (2012) Armed Conflicts, 1946–2011. *Journal of Peace Research* **49**(4), 565–75. https://doi.org/10.1177/0022343312452421.

Torres-Rivas E. and Arévalo de León B. (1999) *Del conflicto al diálogo: El WSP en Guatemala*. Guatemala: UNRISD.

True J. and Parisi L. (2013) Gender Mainstreaming Strategies in International Governance. In Caglar G., Prugle E. and Zwingel S. (eds.), *Feminist Strategies in International Governance*. Abingdon: Routledge, 37–56.

UCDP (2013) UCDP Battle-Related Deaths Dataset v.5–2013. Uppsala: Uppsala University.

UN Security Council (2014) Resolution 2151. http://unscr.com/files/2014/02151.pdf.

United Nations (2015a) The Challenge of Sustaining Peace: Report of the Advisory Group of Experts for the 2015 Review of the UN Peacebuilding Architecture. www.un.org/pga/wp-content/uploads/sites/3/2015/07/300615_The-Challenge-of-Sustaining-Peace.pdf.

(2015b) Uniting Our Strengths for Peace: Politics, Partnerships and People. www.peaceinfrastructures.org/documents/report-high-level-independent-panel-peace-operations.

(2015c) Agenda for Sustainable Development. https://documents-dds-ny.un.org/doc/UNDOC/GEN/N15/291/89/PDF/N1529189.pdf?OpenElement

UN Special Rapporteur on Human Rights defenders, Mary Lawlor (2021) A_HRC_46_35-EN.Pdf. Promotion and Protection of All Human Rights, Civil, Political, Economic, Social and Cultural Rights, Including the Right to Development Human Rights Council Forty-sixth session Agenda item 3. Geneva: UN Human Rights Council.

Uprimny R. (2003) The Constitutional Court and Control of Presidential Extraordinary Powers in Colombia. *Democratization* **10**(4), 46–69. https://doi.org/10.1080/13510340312331294027.

(2014) The Recent Transformation of Constitutional Law in Latin America: Trends and Challenges. *Texas Law Review* **89**, 1587–609.

Valasek K. (2008) Security Sector Reform and Gender. UN Instraw. www.peacewomen.org/assets/file/PWandUN/UNImplementation/ResearchAndTrainingInstitutions/UNISTRAW/uninstraw_genderandssrtoolkit1_2008.pdf.

Vries H. de and Wiegink N. (2011) Breaking up and Going Home? Contesting Two Assumptions in the Demobilization and Reintegration of Former Combatants. *International Peacekeeping* **18**(1), 38–51. https://doi.org/10.1080/13533312.2011.527506.

Wæver O. (2003) Peace and Security: Two Concepts and Their Relationship. In Guzzini S. and Jung D. (eds.), *Contemporary Security Analysis and Copenhagen Peace Research*. London: Routledge, 53–65.

Walby S. (2013) Violence and Society: Introduction to an Emerging Field of Sociology. *Current Sociology* **61**(2), 95–111. https://doi.org/10.1177/0011392112456478.

Walter B. (2002) *Committing to Peace: The Successful Settlement of Civil Wars*. Princeton: Princeton University Press.

(2004) Does Conflict Beget Conflict? Explaining Recurring Civil War. *Journal of Peace Research* **41**(3), 371–88. https://doi.org/10.1177/0022343304043775.

Wood E. J. (2008) The Social Processes of Civil War: The Wartime Transformation of Social Networks. *Annual Review of Political Science* **11**, 539–61.

Cambridge Elements

International Relations

About the Series

The Cambridge Elements Series in International Relations publishes original research on key topics in the field. The series includes manuscripts addressing international security, international political economy, international organizations, and international relations.

Cambridge Elements

International Relations

Elements in the Series

Social Media and International Relations
Sarah Kreps

International Norms, Moral Psychology, and Neuroscience
Richard Price and Kathryn Sikkink

Across Type, Time and Space: American Grand Strategy in Comparative Perspective
Peter Dombrowski and Simon Reich

Contestations of the Liberal International Order
Fredrik Söderbaum, Kilian Spandler, Agnese Pacciardi

Domestic Interests, Democracy, and Foreign Policy Change
Brett Ashley Leeds, Michaela Mattes

Token Forces: How Tiny Troop Deployments Became Ubiquitous in UN Peacekeeping
Katharina P. Coleman, Xiaojun Li

The Dual Nature of Multilateral Development Banks
Laura Francesca Peitz

Peace in Digital International Relations
Oliver P. Richmond, Gëzim Visoka, Ioannis Tellidis

Regionalized Governance in the Global South
Brooke Coe, Kathryn Nash

Digital Globalization
Stephen Weymouth

After Hedging: Hard Choices for the Indo-Pacific States between the US and China
Kai He, Huiyun Feng

Building Pathways to Peace: State–Society Relations and Security Sector Reform
Nadine Ansorg, Sabine Kurtenbach

A full series listing is available at: www.cambridge.org/EIR

Milton Keynes UK
Ingram Content Group UK Ltd.
UKHW020048021223
433466UK00001B/2

9 781009 462662